EDUCATION AT A DISTANCE

EDUCATION AT A DISTANCE:
From Issues to Practice

Edited by
D. Randy Garrison
and
Doug Shale

Robert E. Krieger Publishing Company
Malabar, Florida
1990

Original Edition 1990

Printed and Published by
ROBERT E. KRIEGER PUBLISHING COMPANY, INC.
KRIEGER DRIVE
MALABAR, FLORIDA 32950

Library of Congress Cataloging-in-Publication Data
Education at a distance : from issues to practice / edited by D. Randy
  Garrison and Doug Shale.—Original ed.
      p.   cm.
    ISBN 0-89464-451-3 (alk. paper)
    1. Distance education—United States. 2. University extension- -United States. I.
Garrison, D. R. (D. Randy), 1945-
    II. Shale, Doug.
    LC5805.E38 1990
    378'.03—dc20   89-49284
                                                        CIP

10   9   8   7   6   5   4   3   2

CONTENTS

Contributors   vii

Preface   ix

1 Introduction 1
   Doug Shale and D. Randy Garrison

2 Origins of Distance Education in the United States 7
   Sheila Sherow and Charles A. Wedemeyer

3 Education and Communication 23
   Doug Shale and D. Randy Garrison

4 Communications Technology 41
   D. Randy Garrison

5 Media and Instructional Methods 53
   Bill Winn

6 Instructional Development Concerns 67
   Erv Schieman

7 Course Creation Issues in Distance Education 77
   Mavis Kelly

8 Audio Teleconferencing Design and Delivery 101
   D. Randy Garrison

9 The Integration of Video-Based Instruction 109
   Charlotte Gunawardena

10 A New Framework and Perspective 123
   D. Randy Garrison and Doug Shale

11 Blurring the Boundaries: Parity and Convergence 135
   Fred Jevons

CONTRIBUTORS

THE EDITORS

RANDY GARRISON is the former Director of Distance Education at The University of Calgary and is currently Associate Dean, Research and Development, in the Faculty of Continuing Education. In addition to his practical experience he has numerous publications on distance education including a book titled *Understanding Distance Education*. He has also published widely in the field of adult education and his current interests center around the teaching-learning transaction and critical thinking.

DOUG SHALE is an Analyst in the Office of Institutional Analysis at The University of Calgary. He has had extensive experience working in various aspects of the development, delivery and administration of distance education. He has published widely on a range of issues and topics in distance education but has a particular interest in the governance and administration of higher distance education.

THE CONTRIBUTORS

MAVIS KELLY has been actively involved in distance education in Australia since 1977, at Deakin University and the University of Queensland and she has served as President of the Australian and South Pacific External Studies Association. She has written extensively on distance education and has been consulting internationally in this field.

CHARLOTTE GUNAWARDENA is an assistant professor of distance education at the Department of Learning Technologies, College of Education, University of New Mexico. She was formerly a Kellogg Research Fellow at the Oklahoma Research Center for Continuing Professional and Higher Education at the University of Oklahoma.

BILL WINN is Professor of Education at the University of Washington in Seattle. He has published extensively in the area of instructional systems technology and his work is widely recognized. He has served as Editor of *Educational Communication and Technology Journal*.

ERV SCHIEMAN is Associate Professor in the Department of Curriculum and Instruction, Faculty of Education at The University of Calgary. His current interests in distance education include assessing the effectiveness of distance education methods for delivering courses to rural high schools, and developing courses in distance education to be delivered at a distance as part of a Masters of Education program.

FRED JEVONS is currently Professor and Director of the Institute for Science and Technology at Murdoch University in Western Australia. He was the founding Vice-Chancellor of Deakin University, subsequently becoming an Emeritus Professor at Deakin.

CHARLES WEDEMEYER has had a long and highly regarded association with the development of distance education, not just in the United States but internationally as well. Professor Wedemeyer is currently the William H. Lighty Professor of Education (Emeritus) at the University of Wisconsin.

SHEILA SHEROW is a recent graduate from the Adult Education program at Pensylvania State University. She is currently a Research Associate with the Institute for the study of Adult Literacy in the College of Education at Pennsylvania State University and is involved with looking at how distance education systems can be used to support literacy instruction in rural areas of Pennsylvania.

PREFACE

The current enormous interest in distance education is due in large measure to the appeal that it has to a very broadly based constituency. It seems to have something to offer to almost everyone. The technological hardware of distance education is probably the most obvious and glamorous of the many faces of distance education. Consequently a substantial, probably disproportionate amount of interest generated in distance education has to do with: television; satellites which, although they are strictly delivery support mechanisms, are often spoken of as though they constitute a form of distance education in themselves; teleconferencing and related enhancements, one aspect of which may be satellite carriage; and computers in a variety of functional forms ranging from computer assisted learning to computer conferencing (among others).

Distance education is highly fragmented both in concept and application. This represents both a problem and a challenge to those working at the enterprise. One of the difficulties is that distance education appears to be such a mishmash of ideas and practice that it is difficult to see sufficient unity to support a concerted, coherent advancement of the field. Another problem is that without a strong conceptual basis, distance education will continue to struggle for a "parity of esteem" (Jevons, 1984) with the traditional academic community. For a number of those working in distance education, one avenue of redress has been to attempt to establish that distance education is a discipline and, by implication, deserves the same status as other disciplines. Several attempts have been made to establish the principle (e.g., Holmberg, 1986) but the arguments have not been compelling and the principle clearly has not taken hold. There is so little that is unique to distance education that no independent theory exists to distinguish it. Instead, we find the field comprised of bits and pieces begged, borrowed and stolen from elsewhere. One finds distance education appears in other established fields such as: communications, media, technology, instructional design/ technology, adult and continuing education, nontraditional education, education, (educational) psychology, and so on. Conversely, looking at the published work on distance education, a lot of it appears in journals corresponding to these areas, clearly because it fits well there. Even much of what is printed in designated distance education publications could fit into other journals. With the exception of a number of conceptual papers, what remains is frequently descriptive accounts of "here is how we do distance education." This is not to denigrate such accounts, but merely to indicate that they are not a sufficient basis on which to argue for a comprehensive characterization of distance education.

A major purpose of this book is to bring these different ways of viewing distance education together. To show that a conceptual integrity can unify the apparent diversity, we assume the aim of distance education to be extending access to education to those people who, for one reason or another, cannot avail themselves of the traditional forms.

While education and the noncontiguous relationship between teacher and learner are concomitant characteristics of distance education, we take the view that we are concerned above all with the education of learners who just happen to be physically separate from a teacher. In this context, we consider a defining characteristic of education to be interactive communication between student and teacher. This implies that there must be an opportunity not only for transmitting information from teacher to student, but also that the converse may occur with the result of sustained interaction being a development of knowledge and understanding in the student and potentially in the teacher as well. For this reason, we restrict our attention in the book to "formal" education, understanding that formal education depends on some intervention by an institutionally designated teacher. This means, then, that we will not consider within our ambit the vast and amorphous body of informal education which arguably constitutes the bulk of peoples' learning.

We have also decided to restrict the scope of the book to "higher" distance education since this is the general area where there has been an explosive growth. We exclude the *substantial* worlds of elementary/ secondary correspondence education, proprietary correspondence study (by which we mean correspondence study at all levels sponsored as a business venture), and a variety of other specialized operations. We feel that the context of these operations is sufficiently different from the "usual" form of higher distance education that it ought to be treated separately.

We will also declare as falling outside of the ambit of distance education, those activities in which teachers are transported physically to teach students in their local communities. Since teachers and students meet face-to-face, the instructional process is fundamentally the same as if the students actually were attending an institution, and the instructional challenge of bridging the noncontiguous relationship of teacher and student characteristic of distance education is absent.

The book will be of interest to a wide range of educators who may or may not have knowledge of, or experience in, the field of distance education. It is meant to be of particular interest and value to those educators in adult higher education who are considering the delivery of curricula/programs at a distance.

OVERVIEW OF CONTENTS

The book is broadly organized according to two major themes—one, concerned with broader conceptual ideas and structural issues, is addressed in Chapters 1 through 5. Chapters 6 through 9 build on the framework established in the first five chapters and discuss various instructional methods and practical issues essential to the concept of education at a distance. Chapters 10 and 11 return to conceptual issues introduced in the first five chapters in an attempt to build toward a new basis for thinking about distance education.

Chapter 1 provides an overview of distance education and the themes found throughout the book. In Chapter 2, Sherow and Wedemeyer outline the historical roots of distance education in the United States. They discuss the evolution of the technology of delivering education at a distance as well as the various institutions that came into being in the United States to serve the distance learner.

Chapter 3 provides the conceptual framework and perspective in which distance education is viewed and interpreted throughout the book. The point is made that education is more than information transfer and therefore distance education is more than packaged information. The chapter explicates the educational transaction by analyzing the communication process and the importance of understanding various modes of communication when designing education at a distance. The focus is upon the necessity of two-way communication.

Chapter 4 moves from the all important transactional aspect of education at a distance to the structural means of supporting the communication process. The purpose of this chapter is to establish a basis upon which to evaluate and select technologies for delivering education at a distance.

Chapter 5 provides an important introduction to instructional media and methods from the perspective of delivering education at a distance. This complex and often confusing area is presented skillfully by Bill Winn who suggests some practical guidance in understanding and using media for instruction. In Chapter 6, Erv Schieman provides an overview of instructional development concerns. He discusses specific design issues from a broad model of instructional development and describes their relationship to distance education.

In Chapter 7, Mavis Kelly moves to a discussion of course creation issues from the perspective of distance education ranging from larger planning issues including infrastructure, student support, and media use to the production of instructional packages. Balancing the emphasis on print materials in Kelly's chapter, Chapter 8 provides an overview of planning and instructional issues facing the distance educator who may be considering audio teleconferencing as a technology of delivery. Charlotte Gunawardena, in Chapter 9, provides an overview of integrating video in the design of instruction at a distance. A detailed and thoughtful model is presented as a guide to help students learn from video instruction and how to integrate it with other materials.

The main part of the book concludes in Chapter 10 with a discussion of the major themes identified in the preceding chapters. In particular, themes that are seen as being of concern in the future are addressed. Chapter 11 is a forward looking view of distance education provided by Fred Jevons. He discusses boundaries between traditional and distance education based upon four factors and then suggests why they are becoming blurred.

ACKNOWLEDGMENTS

The view of distance education found in this book was the result of a truly collaborative process between the editors. Through a sustained dialogue over several years the assumptions of distance education were constantly challenged and alternative perspectives proposed. The process in which the editors engaged over this time modeled the educational transaction advocated and described in the book. Given this developmental process, it must be emphasized that the order of names in no way reflects a disproportionate contribution on the part of the editors.

We must also extend our gratitude and sincere thanks to the other authors who contributed to this book. Their knowledge and insight into the design and development of instruction at a distance was invaluable.

Finally, we hope that the book lives up to our expectations and is a useful resource for those working or interested in education at a distance.

CHAPTER 1

INTRODUCTION

Doug Shale and D. Randy Garrison

The growth of university level distance education in recent times has been striking with regard to both the number of students undertaking study at a distance and the numbers of institutions providing distance education. Moreover, this phenomenon transcends national boundaries and to a remarkable extent it is a truly international event. Interestingly enough, though, there has been substantial variation in the ways nations have chosen to respond to the demand for university distance education. In recent times, for example, there has been an almost explosive increase internationally in newly established universities that are dedicated to distance education—the Open University of Britain being the prototypical example. In Australia and New Zealand, university distance education has had a long and venerable tradition as "external studies," a distance education function that is formally integrated by regulation in the operations of some conventional universities. In North America, and particularly in Canada, varieties are numerous, with dedicated distance education institutions (such as Athabasca University and the Open Learning Agency) coexisting with external studies-like operations such as the University of Waterloo Correspondence program—and both of these are surrounded by a melange of distance education courses provided more or less in the context of continuing education at conventional universities.

The tradition in the United States has yet another flavor. Where a dedicated institutional response has occurred, it has occasionally taken the form of a consortium (for example, the now defunct University of Mid-America, and the National Technological University); or it has taken a form that views education in a nontraditional way as, for example, was the case for Nova University; or it may be a hybrid form of conventional course-based distance education and nontraditional education, such as the Empire State College concept. But perhaps the bulk of university distance education emanates from the continuing education function within universities. However, the boundaries around what constitutes university distance education in the United States seems to be considerably more blurred than elsewhere in the world.

DISTANCE EDUCATION IN TRANSITION

The remarkable success of a remarkable institution, the British Open University (BOU), both launched and marked the advent of the "new wave" of distance education that has had such a pronounced effect on the international higher education world.

The open education movement which provided the philosophical underpinnings of the BOU had been around and in the making for some while prior to the creation of the BOU. However, the success of the BOU gave the rest of the world a practical model and an astonishing demonstration of the success of the open education concept. In short order, the BOU became a lodestone for distance education. The lessons of the BOU were too substantial and obvious for the rest of the world to remain oblivious or unheeding. Within 15 years, some 18 other open universities appeared in 16 nations around the world (Holmberg, 1986).

It is the rare educational institution that has not been touched by distance education in one way or another these days, either on the demand or supply side for the kinds of institutions alluded to above, or by the delivery methods through which distance education is often better known. What is often called the hardware for delivering instruction—satellite and cable based television, computer networks, and such—is available to virtually all educational institutions. Moreover, complete multimediated courses (frequently telecourses) are readily available and are often actively marketed to institutions. The increasing need for education of those who cannot obtain it in the traditional way, and the ease of acquiring the means of distance education has, quite naturally, lead to institutional interest where previously there may have been little or none. No doubt the glamour and the high profile associated with the high tech side of distance education has also had substantial allure. Ironically, this apparent easy availability of course packages can be a threat to the academic regard held for distance education—a threat that is exacerbated by the inconsistency of vendors purveying the courseware.

It would be instructive to have a Domesday Book of the distance education activities that exist at the present time. We might all be staggered at the number of institutions around the world that are involved in distance education and at how many students are served. Such inventories have been attempted from time to time but have been less than definitive. One of the difficulties is in deciding what is (and is not) distance education, even in the relatively constrained context of higher, university education. For a variety of reasons the definitions offered thus far have not been particularly satisfactory.

Problems of definition notwithstanding, various attempts have been made to quantify the phenomenon of distance education. For example, Beaudoin writing in 1985 stated that some 55 million Americans took correspondence courses in the 50 years since the establishment of the National Home Study Council in 1926. He also estimated that some 3 million were studying by mail in 1985. Markowitz, writing in 1983, estimated that some 70 conventional institutions in the United States offer courses to an approximate total of 150,000 students. Kaye (1988) reported that the International Council for Distance Education estimated that there were currently 10 million students doing degree courses at a distance in the world. Kay cites Ilyin (1983) as reporting there are 1,200 distance teaching institutions in the USSR with some 1.5 million students taking higher education courses at a distance. Yu Xu (1986) is cited as reporting 40 percent (or about 1 million) of China's university population were taking courses at a distance, and roughly one-third of these took their courses in conjunction with the Radio and Television University of China. Not surprisingly this scale of operation has counterparts in other Asian countries. The Sukhothai Thammathirat Open University of Thailand expects to attain a target of 500,000 university-level students by 1990 (Srisa-an, 1984). The Universitas Terbuka, established in Indonesia in 1984, reported enrolling 60,000 students from a total of 250,000 applications in its first year (Kaye, 1988). In the Republic of Korea, the Correspondence University established in 1982 is reported to have some 250,000 students registered in its programs (Kaye, 1988). Similar open university style initiatives have been established in Japan (The University of the Air, 1985), India (Indira Gandhi National Open University, 1985) and Pakistan (Allama Iqbal Open University, 1974).

In other parts of the world, developments have been equally striking with respect to the establishment of new institutions, even if the numbers of students are somewhat fewer than for the Asian counterparts. The following is an illustrative list drawn from Shale (1987) and Kaye (1988): The British OU, 1969; Universidad Nacional de Educacion, Spain, 1972; Everyman's University, Israel, 1974; FernUniversitat, Federal Republic of Germany, 1974; the Tele-Universite, Canada, 1974; Athabasca University, Canada, 1975; Universidad Nacional Abierta, Venezuela, 1977; Universidad Estatal a Distancia, Costa Rica, 1977; Open Learning Institute, Canada, 1978 (reconstituted as the Open University and Open College of British Columbia, 1987); the Open College, United Kingdom, 1984. The now defunct University of Mid-America and the Nova University may be regarded as manifestations of the open university movement in the United States.

TOWARD A NEW FRAMEWORK

The recent explosion in the development and interest in distance education both in terms of student and institutional participation, has also brought with it heterogeneous methods and delivery systems. Jevons, in the final chapter, believes that this is in fact the hallmark of distance education. However, as a result, by its very nature distance education is no respecter of boundaries whether these relate to the type of clientele or to their geographic location. This institutional and methodological proliferation has made it increasingly difficult to differentiate between conventional and distance education. And it has largely been this phenomenon that has caused us to rethink what distinguishes distance education from other forms of education.

A new framework for distance education which will accommodate the blurring of the boundaries across all forms of higher educational delivery must inevitably, we believe, be based upon an understanding of the essence of the educational transaction. We need to rethink how education *should* be practiced to recapture its essence and approach its ideal and not dwell on how education is currently practiced. In its most fundamental form education is an interaction among teacher, student, and subject content. This transaction in all its complexity, however, is dependent upon sustained two-way communication which provides for the transformation of raw information into knowledge.

Historically, distance education has been characterized as an independent form of study. This situation was necessitated by the limited communications technology of the times. Unfortunately, too often specious attempts were made to turn a serious constraint into an attribute by arguing for the advantages of learner independence in the name of access. While students certainly had access to information largely in print form, some began to question the quality of the educational experience without adequate oppportunity for dialogue and challenging ideas. Today distance educators are beginning to realize that distance education must be responsive to access issues as well as support issues. With the emergence of the new communications technology distance education practitioners are now only limited by their imaginations and a good working philosophy and framework of distance education.

A new framework based upon interdependence can bring prestige and integrity to distance education as a field of study and practice. Although it has been said often that practice must be informed by theory, it still remains true. New directions in the practice of distance education, if they are to be worthwhile and sustainable, will be dependent upon a vision articulated within a coherent and defensible framework. To date it is arguable that such a framework exists in distance education. The need for such a framework becomes evident when we address the complexities of instructional design and delivery at a distance resulting from the many contextual needs and constraints.

Before we can integrate theory and practice we must begin to view distance education as education at a distance. That is, we must begin to place the emphasis on the educational transaction and the interdependence of teacher and student—not on distance and the autonomy of an isolated learner. The framework presented in the following chapters emphasizes interdependence through mediated two-way communication using existing and emerging communications technology. The latter chapters demonstrate in a more concrete manner how we can and do achieve interdependence through a discussion of various design and delivery issues.

However, as we get caught up in all that education at a distance has to offer, we ought to keep in mind the following admonition by Campion and Kelly (1988, p. 31):

Surely the point is, as we move rapidly towards the Twenty First Century, to have a clear philosophy of higher education such that the value of various pedagogies and educational methods can be viewed impartially, and evaluated without their being seen as confined to one mode of education or the other. We need to ask ourselves what arrangement of educational strategies can provide the best access to education (in every sense of the word access) and the best possible use of teaching and learning resources.

Throughout this book, we try to build toward a clearer philosophy of higher education. We hope that what results is a body of advice and principles that can be appealed to in selecting arrangements of educational strategies that do provide "the best access to education."

REFERENCES

Beadoin, M. F. (1985). Independent study: a bum rap for too long. *The Chronicle of Higher Education,* April 24.

Campion, M. and Kelly, M. (1988). Integration of external studies and campus-based education in Australian higher education: the myth and the promise. *Distance Education*, 9(2), 171–201.

Holmberg, B. (1986). *Growth and structure of distance education.* Croom Helm, London.

Kaye, A. (1988). Distance education: the state of the art. *Prospects*, 18 (1), 43–54.

Markowitz, H. (1983). Independent study by correspondence in American universities. *Distance Education*, 4 (2), 147–170.

Shale, D. (1987). Innovation in international higher education: the open universities. *Journal of Distance Education*, 2 (1), 7–26.

Yu Xu (1986). A look into some aspects of distance education in the People's Republic of China. *Distance Education*, 7 (1), 92–105.

CHAPTER 2

ORIGINS OF DISTANCE EDUCATION IN THE UNITED STATES

Sheila Sherow and Charles A. Wedemeyer

In the United States, distance education has taken a flavor quite different from that found in countries that have retained a European influence in their educational institutions (especially, for example, member nations of the British Commonwealth). Education in the United States has always been viewed in an egalitarian spirit prompting the kind of grass roots origins of distance education described in this chapter. Consequently, one finds distance education in the company of the open learning movement and a variety of other nontraditional education forms such as the University Without Walls and independent study programs—the unifying theme being the provision of educational opportunity to those who cannot avail themselves of education provided in the traditional form.

Perhaps this long and evolving grass roots tradition accounts for the fact that distance education in the United States seems to have remained to date largely untouched by the kind of development that has occurred in many other countries throughout the world—most notably the open university movement. This may also explain why compared to other countries, there has been such a paucity of writing about the development of distance education in the United States—a state of affairs that this chapter is meant to address.

ENGLISH EXTENSION MOVEMENT

North American higher education developed with a strong European influence which subsequently affected the establishment of distance education within the university structure. American educators studied German and English educational philosophies, and adapted European principles to the American educational system. The traditional liberal arts curriculum was expanded to include agricultural and industrial education in an attempt to provide scientific solutions to national economic problems. The English extension movement initiated a shift in educational approach from an elitist, scholarly tradition to an extended educational service designed to meet the demands of a labor class. A new type of university education was formed, utilitarian in approach, based on social needs, and not confined to campus study. For the first time, students were provided with alternatives that allowed enrollment at a distance from the campus.

During the mid 1850s, Reverend W. Sewell of Exeter College, Oxford, suggested off-campus study through a system of lectures. James Stuart elaborated on Sewell's ideas and, in 1871, proposed a traveling circuit of lecturing professors who, 18 months later, became the University Extension System at the University of Cambridge (Bittner and Mallory, 1933).

Emergence of English Correspondence Study

Professor Stuart experimented with correspondence study in a series of lecture courses for women. Recognizing the social taboo on personal interviews between men and women as a barrier to effective teaching, Stuart utilized the written word to replace spoken conversation through a correspondence system. He incorporated a syllabus and an examination sheet into printed lessons and conducted instruction through the mail, forming the foundation of the correspondence method still practiced today (Bittner and Mallory, 1933).

Ruskin College in Oxford provided a correspondence system aimed toward students who were unable to attend residential classes but who wanted to continue their education. Off-campus students were sent monthly outlines containing readings, references, essay questions and assignments. Completed work was returned to tutors who corrected assignments and included comments or suggestions. A personal relationship between student and tutor was encouraged through frequent correspondence not limited to routine course work. Similar efforts resulted in the widespread organization of English correspondence programs (Bittner and Mallory, 1933).

AMERICAN ADAPTATION OF THE ENGLISH MODEL

In 1873, inspired by the English "Society for the Encouragement of Home Study," Anna Eliot Ticknor established a similar correspondence system for women which operated out of her home in Boston, Massachusetts. The American "Society to Encourage Studies at Home" enrolled over 7,000 women in its university-level correspondence courses over a period of 24 years, discontinuing its operation in 1897 following Anna Ticknor's death (Ticknor, 1896).

Although Dr. W. R. Harper is credited with the popularization of correspondence instruction within university extension in the United States, Anna Ticknor was a pioneer of the American correspondence method (Mackenzie and Christensen, 1971, p. 71). Ticknor's Society was a correspondence system designed exclusively for women which, in following Stuart's earlier model, attempted to circumvent traditionally female educational barriers through nontraditional methods. The courses were primarily liberal arts subjects but included controversial science courses based on laboratory methods. Although the Society was not affiliated with a university or college, its curriculum was of equal quality and represented a full range of typical college courses. Similar to Ruskin College in method, the Society emphasized a personal student/teacher relationship that was maintained through regular monthly correspondence. Following enrollment procedures that attempted to identify individual student interests, women were assigned to a staff teacher. All subsequent communication was conducted through student/teacher correspondence (Ticknor, 1896).

A "memory note" system was developed within the Society to provide students with a correspondence study technique. The note-taking system proved to be popular as well as effective, and became a key component of the Society's correspondence method. Samples of "memory notes" were submitted with monthly correspondence for corrections and comments. The Society was originally established as a degree program but after two years the program proved to be unsatisfactory and was replaced with a nondegree curriculum that remained popular throughout the Society's operation (Ticknor, 1896).

Institutionalization of Correspondence Instruction

An early American educational institution, the Chautauqua Institute, also offered university-level correspondence study during the late 1800s. The Institute was founded in 1874, as a Summer Assembly to provide training for the improvement of Sunday School teaching. Increasing annual enrolments and growing interest in programming available throughout the year, led to an expansion in the types of programs it offered. In 1878, the first of two correspondence programs was established to provide nondegree but university-level courses. The Chautauqua Literary and Scientific Circle (CLSC) was a planned home reading program based on a college-like curriculum. The CLSC was not intended to substitute for a university education but was designed to be a superficial exposure to traditional liberal arts subjects. Examinations were available for those interested in accumulating credits and diplomas were awarded for successful completion of the four-year cycle of planned study. Its student population was a heterogeneous group of adults located throughout the United States including college graduates, professional people, those with little or no formal schooling, and adults who wished to better themselves through continuing education (Vincent, 1886). Although CLSC readers were representative of the American public, the majority were middle class, working men and women, many of whom formed local reading circles for discussion and debate. From 1880 to the early 1900s enrolments increased nationally and internationally. The first reported CLSC circle outside of the United States was located in Wolsey, Saskatchewan, in 1886.

A college degree Chautauquan correspondence program was established in 1885 through the efforts of Dr. W. R. Harper. The CCLA was granted the power to confer degrees as an official university by the state of New York and continued to do so until 1891. The CCLA operated independent of the Institute with each CCLA professor being responsible for his own course curriculum and administration (Vincent, 1886).

Harper, originally hired by the Institute to teach Hebrew during the Summer Assembly, refined the correspondence method that had originated with the earlier English and American models. His first experiments with correspondence instruction had been attempts to alleviate overcrowded classroom conditions with nonresidential study opportunities. The overwhelmingly positive and enthusiastic responses his first lessons received stimulated his interest in correspondence courses as an effective and valuable method of study. Harper regarded correspondence instruction as an alternative to traditional oral instruction but recognized and emphasized the benefits and limitations of each. His goal was not to replace traditional methods but to provide appropriate and effective alternatives for those students unable to take advantage of residential instruction.

After several unsuccessful attempts to institutionalize his original private correspondence methods, Harper finally developed a system adopted by the Chautauqua Institute in 1885 that became the first publicly announced American correspondence system (Noffsinger, 1926, p. 9). Harper's correspondence method was a three-part system based on Stuart's original model with an additional recitation paper designed to provide two-way communication between student and instructor. The syllabus, or instruction sheet, was mailed weekly to students with assignments. It directed the sequencing of work, explained difficult segments of the lessons and provided review work. Through various types of exercises, the examination paper thoroughly assessed the student's comprehension of the subject (Mackenzie and Christensen, 1971, p. 8).

Writing in the late nineteenth century, Harper believed there were certain weaknesses in distance education that resulted from a lack of contiguous instructor support and motivation (Vincent, 1886). He identified self-directed and autonomous learner characteristics that he believed were necessary for successful correspondence study. On the other hand, Harper recognized the benefits inherent within distance education and supported the view that the correspondence method encouraged a mastery of the subject that residential students seldom experienced. Through required comprehensive written assignments, correspondence students experienced a more independent and complete examination of the topic, which resulted in a more thorough understanding of the subject (Vincent, 1886).

AMERICAN UNIVERSITY EXTENSION

University Extension at Chicago

The University of Chicago opened in 1892 with a five division organization adapted from Chautauquan educational principles. Three of the divisions were totally new to university structure, one of which was an extension division with plans for a correspondence department (Noffsinger, 1926, p. 18; Bittner and Mallory, 1933, p. 19). The University's first correspondence student enrolled in October, 1892, meeting the eligibility requirements that mandated a minimum age of 21, and verification that residential study was not possible (Noffsinger, 1926, p. 19; Bittner and Mallory, 1933, p. 19).

There were two methods of instruction available at Chicago: formal lesson sheets sent to students, and informal correspondence conducted through department heads. Traditional academic requirements were modified to fit the needs of extension study and to accommodate a heterogeneous group of students pursuing education for varying reasons and purposes (Noffsinger, 1926, p. 20). Harper duplicated a traditional university curriculum within the home study department similar to the liberal arts subjects offered by the CCLA and Ticknor's Society. In 1892, 82 University of Chicago students were studying 39 different courses by correspondence, instructed by 23 professors (Bittner and Mallory, 1933, p. 22). It wasn't until the University of Wisconsin became reinvolved in correspondence instruction in 1906 that a shift from an exclusively academic to a primary vocational and practical curriculum was evident (Mackenzie, Christensen and Rigby, 1968, p. 30; Reber, 1914, pp. 6, 26).

Illinois Wesleyan

Illinois Wesleyan was established as a Methodist endowed denominational institution and granted a charter with the power to confer degrees by the state of Illinois in 1853. Twenty years later the university began to offer nonresident credit and noncredit correspondence courses to help students prepare for university exams. Admission requirements were based on preparatory credits, and course study was evaluated on the same basis as residential course work (Bittner and Mallory, 1933, p. 15). Following criticisms and debates regarding the equivalency of standards for resident and nonresident students, the University Senate of Methodist Institutions decreed that all colleges within the federation had four years in which to phase out their correspondence programs. Consequently, Illinois Wesleyan discontinued its correspondence program in 1906 (Mackenzie, Christensen and Rigby, 1968, p. 26).

The Correspondence University

The Correspondence University in Ithaca, New York was formed in 1883 by 32 university professors representing different colleges and universities, including; Harvard, Johns Hopkins and University of Wisconsin. Their common aim was to supplement college instructions with correspondence study. Unlike the CCLA and Illinois Wesleyan, the Correspondence University was not chartered as an official university and did not have the power to confer degrees (Mackenzie, Christensen and Rigby, 1968, p. 26). Its curriculum was typical of a liberal arts college, aimed toward the needs of college graduates, professionals, teachers and officers in the armed forces. The University attempted to uphold traditional standards and requirements but only honorary recognitions could be earned (Noffsinger, 1926). Its program lasted only a short time due to poor administration and lack of organization.

University of Wisconsin Extension and Correspondence Study

The University of Wisconsin first proposed correspondence study in its 1889–1890 catalog as a function of university extension (Wedemeyer and Allen, 1957, p. 19). The catalog compared the English extension movement with its American version, defining the major difference to be an English cultural curriculum approach as opposed to the Wisconsin vocational and industrial course emphasis (Wedemeyer and Allen, 1957, p. 19). Private correspondence study at university level was available at Wisconsin in 1891, although correspondence instruction was viewed as an inferior method of study valuable only to those unable to attend residential courses (Wedemeyer and Allen, 1957, p. 20).

Preparation of correspondence lessons and course administration were responsibilities of University faculty members. Student fees were paid directly to individual professors in reimbursement of costs incurred. Faculty enthusiasm for correspondence instruction was limited due to the heavy work burden it put on professors and the lack of administrative support to carry it financially. In 1896, a correspondence system was announced that included 63 courses that earned credits toward bachelor's, master's, and doctor's degrees (Wedemeyer and Allen, 1957, p. 26). Unfortunately, a lack of funds and administrators in addition to growing concerns over the quality of correspondence instruction affected the promotion and subsequent continuance of correspondence instruction. The extensive time needed for correcting lessons often necessitated using advanced students as instructors which led to skepticism regarding the creditability of correspondence instruction in relation to residential study. The emergence of free traveling libraries and county normal schools offered the public new alternatives and correspondence study enrollments began to decrease (Wedemeyer and Allen, 1957, p. 28). By 1900, Wisconsin's correspondence study courses had been allowed to phase out (Wedemeyer and Allen, 1957, p. 30).

Van Hise at Wisconsin

In 1903, Charles Van Hise was elected President of the University of Wisconsin and, in 1906, he announced the reemergence of correspondence instruction (Wedemeyer and Allen, 1957, p. 33; Mackenzie, Christensen and Rigby, 1968, p. 29). Van Hise realized the success of commercial correspondence schools and encouraged Wisconsin citizens to invest in their own system which would include languages, literature, political economy, political science, history, sociology, mathematics, pure sciences and applied sciences (Wedemeyer and Allen, 1957, p. 34–35). In compliance with the University's land-grant appropriation provisions, courses in vocational and industrial subjects were also included, enabling the public to choose an appropriate course of study. Realizing that the weakness of Wisconsin's original correspondence system was largely due to its lack of administrative support, Van Hise appointed William Lighty as full-time Director of Correspondence Instruction. Lighty favored a cultural curriculum that neglected the vocational and practical objectives of the University (Wedemeyer and Allen, 1957, p. 41). Van Hise, in an attempt to provide leadership in agricultural and industrial education, appointed Louis Reber from the Pennsylvania State College as Director of Wisconsin's Extension Division (Wedemeyer and Allen, 1957, p. 42). Within a year of his appointment, Reber established an extension staff separate from residential administration with full-time correspondence instructors. The potential conflict between Lighty's cultural approach and Reber's vocational goals never materialized. Reber allowed Lighty to develop liberal arts and University credit courses while he took responsibility for the preparation and administration of industrial training correspondence courses (Wedemeyer and Allen, 1957, p. 44).

Lighty founded the National University Extension Association (NUEA) in 1915, and was elected its president in 1927. His administration influenced a change in attitude toward correspondence instruction creating a more respected view of its academic potentials. Lighty's contributions to correspondence instruction were recognized internationally. Australian, German and Russian educators traveled to Wisconsin to study his administrative and instructional methods.

The renewed Wisconsin correspondence study method included a consecutive series of lessons exclusively or partially conducted through correspondence. There were two levels of instruction offered; one resembled the CLSC planned readings with guided study outlines appropriate for groups and clubs and a second more advanced level, which took precedence over the less formal, was based on structured assignments and examinations (Mackenzie, Christensen and Rigby, 1968, p. 19). By 1914, there were 31 full-time correspondence instructors and 35 part-time teachers within the Extension Division; 18 members of the resident faculty carried correspondence courses and 37 others supported correspondence study in various ways (Reber, 1914, p. 14)

Louis Reber's 1914 University Extension Report

In 1914, the U.S. Bureau of Education published Reber's report on University Extension in the United States in which he reported 32 American colleges and universities with correspondence programs operating out of their extension divisions (p. 20). Reber (1914, p. 5) attributed the original development of American university extension to an 1887 American Library Association address that generated interest in the English extension movement as an adjunct to the city library. He recognized the Chautauquan influence on university correspondence study both in philosophy and mission (1914, p. 5). Between 1887 and the establishment of the University of Chicago in 1892, Reber (1914, p. 6) reported 28 states and territories with unorganized forms of extension. University extension work remained unorganized until the establishment of the University of Chicago's and the University of Wisconsin's extension divisions. Between 1892 and the reemergence of correspondence study at Wisconsin in 1906, 12 additional universities organized extension divisions (Reber, 1914, p. 6).

American correspondence study programs differed from English instruction in curriculum. Universities in the United States offered primarily agricultural and industrial courses with limited liberal arts subjects as opposed to exclusively traditional academic courses. Opinions on the effectiveness of correspondence study varied. Some American educators condemned it as inferior to traditional university level instruction, claiming that correspondence programs actually detracted from the institution's academic prestige. Typically, early correspondence instruction had been the responsibility of individual faculty members on a fee basis but by 1914 administrative support was evident in the appointment of staff members and appropriated funding.

During the 1913–1914 academic year, correspondence courses carried a wide range of credit standards and requirements within equally differing administrative structures (Reber, 1914, p. 21). The vast majority of the institutions relied on resident and part-time staff to prepare, instruct and administer correspondence programs. Cultural and liberal arts courses remained popular and practical training, vocational and agricultural course enrollments increased. Credit and noncredit courses were available. Some institutions enrolled a large percentage of noncredit seeking students while others, like the University of Chicago, provided more credit courses (Reber, 1914, p. 26).

Although critics of correspondence study feared that students would take advantage of the method as an easy means of attaining credit, Reber (1914, p. 26) reported that statistics indicated that correspondence students achieved higher than average academically when enrolled in residential courses. Reber also noted that, with the exception of the University of Wisconsin, few texts had been written exclusively for correspondence study.

Correspondence study was the first form of distance education, beginning with private tutoring by means of written correspondence sent through the mail. It was later institutionalized as a function of university extension. The English correspondence method became the foundation for the later American versions with the basic elements of course design remaining relatively unchanged.

Between 1958 and 1959 nearly 2 million Americans were taught by correspondence instruction. One year later 123,000 Canadian enrollments were recorded (Erdos, 1967, p. 4). Teaching by print has remained the most popular distance education medium either as the primary instructional method or supplemental to other media.

Rapid advancements in technology resulting from World War I and World War II both stimulated and retarded the growth of distance education. The development of radio and television was primarily due to war-related efforts. Consequently, immediate civilian use was limited due to military priorities.

Educational Radio

In addition to his duties as Director of Correspondence Instruction, Lighty pioneered educational radio with the establishment of the first university radio station, WHA, the "School of the Air." In 1920, the University of Wisconsin had one of three experimental radio stations in the United States involved in testing radio's effectiveness as a public broadcast medium. It was operated by the University's Physics Department to broadcast weather and market reports. Lighty became the first WHA Program Director with the intention to eventually supplement correspondence study and other extension activities with educational radio programming. Through his work with the NUEA, Lighty helped organize the National Association of Educational Broadcasters (NAEB).

The University of Iowa, California State University, Florida State University, Indiana State University, Nebraska State University and the Massachusetts Division of University Extension were early pioneers in combining correspondence instruction with educational radio programming (Noffsinger, 1927, p. 26).

During the 1930s and early 1940s, approximately 20 educational radio stations were broadcasting in the AM band (Chester and Garrison, 1950, p. 201). Many were affiliated with state universities and won awards for superior programming, including Wisconsin, Iowa, Minnesota, Ohio, and Oklahoma (Chester and Garrison, 1950, p. 201). The actual audiences, in comparison to the popularity of the commercial station audiences and in comparison with the potential audiences, were small but their broadcasts covered approximately half of the American people which, in comparison with other educational media, was quite impressive (Chester and Garrison, 1950, p. 201).

By 1956 most educational stations belonged to the National Association of Educational Broadcasters (NAEB) located at the University of Illinois-Urbana and supported by the W. K. Kellogg Foundation and the Ford Foundation's Fund for Adult Education (Chester and Garrison, 1950, p. 202). The Association operated a tape network to provide tape recordings of superior educational programs to member stations and commissioned the production of special educational programs.

The earliest Canadian educational radio was aimed toward the needs of the rural population during the 1930s. Dr. M. M. Coby, at St. Francis Xavier University directed the Antigonish Movement which was based on community education through group study, discussion and action. Radio was adapted to Coby's methods and was utilized by the Workers' Educational Association in 1935 to broadcast rural economic issues (Norquay, 1986, p. 247). In 1937 rural education became a part of the Canadian Broadcasting Corporation (CBC) national network which, through the co-sponsorship of the Canadian Association for Adult Education, began educational radio programming with study materials prepared by MacDonald College.

National Farm Radio Forum was first broadcast in every province on November 10, 1941. Farm Forums were local study and discussion groups of between four and twenty people who met in each other's homes on a weekly basis. Groups were provided with discussion questions prior to broadcasts and were asked to record and submit their answers or comments to the Farm Forum office. The office summarized group answers over the air, answering any questions that might have been submitted by students (Norquay, 1986, pp. 248–249).

In 1971 Ryerson Open College, inspired by the distance methods of the British Open University, began broadcasting its first course by radio (Norquay, 1986, p. 249).

Television as an Instructional Medium

Between 1948 and 1952, 108 television stations were broadcasting in the United States. Out of these, only WOI-TV in Ames, Iowa was owned by an educational institution, the Iowa State College (Chester and Garrison, 1950, p. 209). Because it was the only station serving a large population in Iowa, WOI-TV carried commercial network entertainment in addition to its own educational programming (Chester and Garrison, 1950, p. 209).

The NAEB and a newly formed Joint Committee for Educational Television (JCET) supported the reservation of educational use of broadcast channels. In 1952, 242 television channels out of 2,053 were reserved for educational groups only. The number was later increased to 252, out of which 168 were UHF assignments (Chester and Garrison, 1950, p. 209). A National Citizen's Commission was formed to mobilize public opinion regarding educational programming.

In 1959 the "Continental Classroom" was broadcast by the University of California supplemented by correspondence study. Physics and chemistry courses were instructed through television broadcasts aided with course syllabi that were sold to persons interested in studying the courses for credit.

However, in general the use of television in distance education throughout the world has remained limited in relation to its educational potential. In 1982 only 2 of 14 open universities established utilized more than 5 hours of television broadcasting a week. The British Open University was broadcasting 35 hours a week and the Chinese Central Television University utilized instructional television 32 hours weekly. Canadian universities have used primarily cable television; the Tele-universite and Athabasca University have averaged between 9 and 12 hours of television broadcasts a week (Bates, 1984, p. 29).

AMERICAN INNOVATIONS IN DISTANCE EDUCATION SYSTEMS

Project AIM, Articulated Instructional Media, was the major American contribution to the establishment of the British Open University, and in a broader sense, to a new type of distance education. Dr. Charles Wedemeyer began work on AIM at the University of Wisconsin in 1964. It was proposed that a unique system be developed for a new type of institution, one that would provide educational opportunities at times and places that were convenient for adults. Distance education was to be made possible through course design utilizing media and technology and would be supported by counseling and resource and learning centers. Innovations in administration and faculty development were seen as imperative to the success of AIM, necessitating retraining in a team approach to instruction. Wedemeyer in 1965 lectured throughout the United Kingdom on the principles behind AIM, focusing on the establishment of a new type of university that would be autonomous in administration and would serve an adult population through correspondence study and other distance media (Wedemeyer, 1984).

Project AIM's mission supported the educational model the British were attempting to build through the establishment of the Open University. (The University of South Africa, the Young-Perraton National Extension College at Cambridge, and the University of New South Wales at Armidale, Australia were also instrumental models in its organization (Wedemeyer, 1984)). The British Open University was established as a multimedia, higher education system providing new opportunities for students who previously had been deprived of educational opportunity due to geographic remoteness, family and occupation responsibilities or physical disability. The Open University was largely influenced by Wedemeyer's work with Project Aim and by postwar developments in cybernetics, systems theory and new educational technology.

The British Open University's influence on distance teaching universities was apparent in the United States as well as internationally. Empire State University, established in 1971 within the State University of New York system, was founded on a mission to develop and provide alternative ways of obtaining off-campus education. The College focuses on four areas: (1) access responsive to student need; (2) content responsive to social, educational and individual need; (3) flexible methods responsive to student need; and (4) continued research in alternative methods, with cost-effectiveness as a significant factor. Regional centers have been established throughout New York, in addition to the Center for Distance Learning that supports guided independent study. The College offers an eclectic assortment of courses and credits through independent or group study. Self-instructional programs, correspondence courses, programmed learning and television courses are available (Raggatt and Harry, 1984, pp. 39–40).

Nova University in Florida has developed a hybrid distance delivery method using a field-based system of local clusters of students that combines formal instruction, independent study and applied research. The program offered through this delivery system is a Doctor of Education with several possible specializations of study within the field of education.

Several universities in the United States have utilized distance education materials developed at the British Open University; Rutgers University, University of Houston, and the University of Maryland have developed programs that are dependent upon Open University instructional materials. Other institutions such as the International University Consortium based at the University of Maryland, have been established to design, prepare and distribute university level instructional materials, the administration of courses remaining the responsibility of individual institutions.

American Cooperative Efforts

The International University Consortium for Telecommunications in Learning (IUC), originally known as the National University Consortium (NUC), was developed by the University of Maryland College University and the Maryland Center for Public Broadcasting. Through funding from the Carnegie Foundation, the IUC was established in 1980 to furnish member universities and colleges, working in partnership with local television stations, with guided study courses of a high academic quality. Courses are based on the British Open University model. Some have been developed by the Open University and others have been produced through the Consortium. All IUC courses include a syllabus, study guide, texts, supplemental media and student assessments. All courses are under the administration of a member institution and are conducted through university faculty and student interaction (Raggatt and Harry, 1984, pp. 52–53).

The National University Teleconferencing Network (NUTN) was organized by members of the NUCEA in 1982 as a cooperative network to provide teleconferencing services for members and external groups. Audio, satellite video and computer conferences with instructional and technical support are available to over 100 higher education institutions. The aim of the NUTN is to reach national audiences with continuing education in an attempt to broaden professional development opportunities. The NUTN operates in cooperation with private industry as with public and private associations that are interested in educational programming (Oberle, 1986).

A second network organization (now defunct), the University of Mid-America (UMA), was a regional institution that provided television courses to seven midwestern states. The participating state universities provided student support, examinations and conferred degrees. Based on similar objectives, the organization of the American Open University was subsequently proposed (Keegan and Rumble, 1982, p. 24).

CONCLUSION

The transformation and gains realized in distance education have been impressive by any standard. However, as mentioned earlier, we would seriously misjudge the nature and potential of distance education if we failed to appreciate the extent to which it has developed within existing educational institutions. This would be particularly so in such countries as the United States, Australia, New Zealand, various African countries, the Soviet Union and South Africa—countries which have substantial numbers of students studying at a distance in courses and programs offered by more or less conventional educational institutions. In a sense, the new distance education institutions proposed to serve a particular clientele and defined a new educational market by virtue of what they have done. Existing distance education providers are instruments through which another face of this demand for distance education is emerging.

The evolution of distance education has expanded the power of the university beyond the traditional classroom. Its history has reflected the changing demands of many societies and has been influenced by increasing industrialization and advancements in technology. As a result, the reality of an individual's undeniable right to learn is more fully achieved.

REFERENCES

Bates, A. (Ed.) (1984). Broadcast Television. In A. Bates (Ed.), *The Role of Technology in Distance Education*. London: Croom-Helm.

Bittner, W., and Mallory, H. (1933). *University teaching by mail*. New York: The Macmillan Company.

Chester, G., and Garrison, G. (1956). *Television and radio*. New York: Appleton-Century-Crofts, Inc.

Erdos, R. (1967). *Teaching by correspondence*. London: Longman, Green & Company.

Keegan, D., and Rumble, G. (1982). *The distance teaching universities*. London: Croom-Helm.

Mackenzie, O., and Christensen, E. (1971). *The changing world of correspondence study*. University Park, Pa.: Pennsylvania State University Press.

Mackenzie, O., Christensen, E., and Rigby, P. (1968). *Correspondence instruction in the United States*. New York: McGraw-Hill Book Company.

Noffsinger, J. S. (1926). *Correspondence schools, lyceums, chautauquas*. New York: The Macmillan Company.

Norquay, M. (1986). Educational radio. In I. Mugridge and D. Kaufman (Eds.), *Distance Education in Canada*. London: Croom-Helm.

Oberle, M. (1986). The national university teleconferencing network. *Teleconference Magazine*, 5,1.

Raggatt, P., and Harry, K. (Eds.) (1986). *Trends in distance education, Part 2*. DERG Papers, No. 10b. Milton Keynes: International Documentation Centre for Distance Learning, November.

Reber, L. (1914). *University extension in the United States.* Washington: Government Printing Office.

Ticknor, A. E. (1896). *The society to encourage studies at home.* Cambridge: Riverside Press.

Vincent, J. H. (1886). *The Chautauqua movement.* Meadville, Pa.: The Chautauqua Press.

Wedemeyer, C., and Allen, C. (1957). *Extending to the people.* Madison, Wisconsin: University of Wisconsin Extension Division.

Wedemeyer, C. (1984). *Preliminary draft.* As submitted Borje Holmberg.

CHAPTER 3

EDUCATION AND COMMUNICATION

Doug Shale and D. Randy Garrison

There is enormous variety in the ways distance education is conducted, in the social and cultural contexts within which it is embedded, and in the organizational forms used to support it. This diversity has resulted in an unusually high degree of fragmentation that encumbers a full appreciation and development of distance education as a "field" of study and practice—even if the return for this fragmentation is the stimulation provided by the variety of all that passes for distance education. A consequence of this fragmentation is that the literature of distance education is replete with ambiguity and dissonance. Ironically, one of the most striking examples of this dissonance is the inability of distance education to define itself satisfactorily to those involved.

The dissonance appears in other forms as well. For example, the issue of independence and interaction (Daniel and Marquis, 1979), or "control" as Garrison and Baynton (1987) characterize it, continues to provoke discussion. Other exchanges regularly occur in the literature over the concepts of learner-centeredness, self-directed learning, independent learning, teaching and learning, formal and informal learning, and so on. At other times, discussions have focussed on the role of technology and the role of the teacher (if there is to be one). It is possible to produce a fairly lengthy list of items that contains such polarized pairings, but the only end to such an activity is likely to be confirmation of what we already know—distance education is indeed a conceptually fragmented field. How, then, are we to find our way through all of this? Is there some unifying theme that can pull together these disparate issues and provide a sense of what distance education is? We think there is, and identifying that theme is the object of this chapter.

DEFINING DISTANCE EDUCATION

Other authors have traced the origins of distance education, describing how it is rooted in the traditions of correspondence study (e.g.,

Holmberg, 1986). In fact, the usual perspective of distance education is as an evolutionary development of correspondence education. Under this view, distance education would be defined by the features that have been characteristically associated with correspondence education, namely:

— the quasi-permanent separation of teacher and learner;
— the influence of an educational organization both in the planning and preparation of learning materials and in the provision of student support services;
— the use of technical media to unite teacher and learner and to carry the content of the course;
— the provision of two-way communication so that the student may benefit from or even initiate dialogue;
— the quasi-permanent absence of the learning group throughout the length of the learning process so that people are usually taught as individuals and not in groups, with the possibility of occasional meetings for didactic and socialization purposes.

(Keegan, 1986)

Keegan (1986) has also noted "two socio-cultural determinants which are both necessary pre-conditions and necessary consequences of distance education" (p. 50); (namely):

— the presence of more industrialized features than in conventional oral education.
— the "privatization of institutional learning."

There have been a number of critiques of this point of view of distance education (for example, Ljosa, 1988). One problem with this characterization of distance education is that it does not fit well the variety of educational activities that are generally recognized as distance education—for instance, teleconferencing, which has been a popular method of delivery for distance education for a long time, does not fit such a description of distance education. Moreover, as various authors have noted (for example, Garrison and Shale, 1987), the fit will only get worse as the technologies and the related infrastructures evolve. The description also does not accommodate hybrid forms of study based on both conventional, face-to-face instruction and distance delivered instruction. Another problem with characterizing distance education as Keegan and Holmberg have done is that the description confuses causes with effects. For example, the classical form of correspondence study had to rely on the mail to bridge the physical separation of teacher and learner. Consequently, the "instruction" had to be embodied in a set of print-based materials. As time passed and the technology for publishing print-based materials advanced, a significant portion of the operations of distance education institutions was associated with the increasingly sophisticated, industrialized process of producing and distributing course materials. However, it is important to recognize that the "industrialization" of the process is simply a consequence of attempting to produce correspondence materials more efficiently. A problem arises when we start to regard "industrialization" as a defining characteristic because to do so presumes that correspondence methods are the only way to bridge the physical separation of teacher and learner and, of course, they are not.

The root of much of the problem is that many of the so-called "definitions" of distance education are the result of a morphologically-oriented, classificatory approach. That is, they have been based primarily on a study of the form and structure of *existing* forms of distance education without sufficient regard for their functional bases. This preoccupation with "how" distance education does what it does has had significant implications. For one thing, it causes us to be too bounded by past practices as we think about what distance education is and what it might become. For another, it leads to an undue emphasis on the "distance" aspect of distance education. This, in turn, perpetuates an undue concern for the form that distance education takes and neglects the critical issue that distance education should be about "education" with the morphological constraints arising from distance being simply a physical and therefore methodological constraint.

To avoid the restrictive trap of describing distance education based upon its existing forms and structures, Garrison and Shale (1987) propose using a set of criteria against which an educational activity may be compared. The essential criteria they suggest for characterizing the distance education process are:

1. Distance education implies that the majority of educational communication between (among) teachers and student(s) occurs noncontiguously.
2. Distance education must involve two-way communication between (among) teacher and student(s) for the purpose of facilitating and supporting the educational process.
3. Distance education uses technology to mediate the necessary two-way communication.

(Garrison & Shale, 1987, p. 11)

An assumption underlying these criteria is that an educational experience requires two-way communication between teacher and student. Moreover, since teacher and student are generally in a non-contiguous relationship, then mediated communication is a necessity. Also, it should be emphasized that this approach to characterizing distance education does not necessarily preclude conventional face to face interaction.

Distance education has made great advances in the past two decades and the practical realities that have had to be faced have helped to clear away some of the conceptual ambiguities that have existed. However, in our view, an abiding resolution to the problem of conceptual ambiguity of distance education is to regard it as education—and not to hold the incidental consideration of the physical separation of teacher and student as a defining point of differentiation. The implications of such an approach will be explored somewhat in subsequent sections of this chapter—and, indeed, in subsequent chapters of this book. However, there is a philosophical mistake that underlies the point of view of distance education that uses distance as a distinguishing/defining feature—and it needs to be explored and exorcised as a separate, albeit somewhat redundant, argument.

DISTANCE EDUCATION AS PROCESS

The nub of this philosophical mistake is captured in a translation by John Baath of some material published in the prospectus of the Toussaint-Langenscheidt correspondence school in Berlin (Methode Toussaint-Langenscheidt, 1901, p. 10 as translated by Baath, 1975, p. 62 and cited in Holmberg, 1986, p. 7). The authors of the prospectus in remarking that students were given opportunities to submit questions, observed: ". . . it would hardly be necessary, since everything is fully explained in the course." This philosophical predisposition in the correspondence view of distance education has persisted and exists even to present day. For example, regarding distance education as an industrialized form of education naturally and easily leads to a regard for education as a commodity to be "packaged" and distributed (and consumed by a learner). And from there, it is just a small step to move to a "technology of education" or instructional design point of view which assumes ". . . it should have been possible to make written materials so effective that face-to-face contact would have only a 'remedial' role, as a final 'control procedure' for the problem student . . ." (Harris, 1987; pp. 52–53). This issue was a source of considerable debate as the Open University developed (Harris,

1987) and also appeared as an issue in other, similar circumstances (for example, Athabasca University in Canada).

The implications of such a point of view are enormous. For example, under this point of view, instruction reduces to packaging knowledge, literally reducing teaching to telling, and learning reduces to the largely solitary consumption of such packaged knowledge on the part of the learner. From there, it is an easy step to believing that the role of the teacher is that of a utility, a resource that can be used and then dispensed with, that the "essence" of the teacher can exist as a "product" and that students have only to partake of the package to become "educated."

This is why there is disagreement on the role of the teacher in distance education. If we assume that knowledge can be packaged and that education consists of transmitting such "packaged knowledge," then there is no role for a teacher other than the packaging of the material, or the remediation referred to in the OU debate. By extension, it follows that packaged printed materials, television courses, and so on, do the teaching and the student in receiving the material and "processing" through it becomes educated. A number of problems arise from regarding education (let alone distance education) in this way. One consequence is that we end up with a very amorphous and nondifferentiated sense of what education is. As Lawson (1974) has pointed out, since any experience has the potential to be a learning situation, the unqualified idea of a learning situation is so general as to be of little use to an educational institution. Education could potentially be anything ranging from reading a book to watching a television program, to walking down the street, to taking a course, and so on. Consequently, we do not have a definition of education that meets the requirements of a definition. Without a common (and unambiguous) definitional base from which to proceed, discussions understandably occur at cross-purposes. At the very least, we need to be able to differentiate between the vast universe of knowledge and understanding consisting of things we come to know by simply living our lives and the admittedly much more constrained universe of knowledge and understanding consisting of what will be called here, "validated" knowledge. The purpose of the second half of this chapter is to attempt such a differentiation and to discuss the implications arising from the conceptualization of education that results.

Another difficulty that occurs because of the conceptual (and actual) separation of subject matter and methods of instruction is that such a view of education is self-limiting. This perspective of education as a "stand alone" activity and students as empty vessels to be filled leads to a representation of distance education as a competitor and a (cheaper, more efficient) alternative to mainstream education. What is wrong with this point of view? The easy answer, of course, is that the concept does not really work in practice. To understand "what is wrong" in a deeper sense, we have to look at the philosophical underpinnings of the world view that would separate the subject matter of instruction from the method of instruction.

Dewey (1917) in exploring the implications of ". . . the connection of subject matter and method with each other" (p. 193) comments:

> The idea that mind and the world of things and persons are two separate and independent realms—a theory which philosophically is known as dualism—carries with it the conclusion that method and subject matter of instruction are separate affairs. Subject matter then becomes a ready-made systematized classification of the facts and principles of the world of nature and man. Method then has for its province a consideration of the ways in which this antecedent subject matter may be best presented to and impressed upon the mind; or, a consideration of the ways in which the mind may be externally brought to bear upon the matter so as to facilitate its acquisition and possession. (p. 193)

Dewey goes on to warn us away from this view, pointing out ". . . that thinking is the method of an educative experience. The essentials of method are therefore identical with the essentials of reflection" (1917, p. 192). One conclusion we can draw from Dewey's position is that any particular rendering of a knowledge package is only one of an indeterminate number of possibilities. Moreover, one could extend the essence of the argument to claim that there will always be sufficient ambiguity, or flexibility in interpreting even a given package (because of interpretations arising from the multitude of assumptions that one always makes in the act of packaging information) that there is no absolute, perfectly replicable, nontrivial set of learning outcomes that result when students interact with it. In short, packaged knowledge as objective knowledge is illusory. Moreover:

> Once the pretense of objectivism is gone we can, as Bernstein (1985) puts it, "dedicate ourselves to the practical task of furthering the type of solidarity, participation, and mutual recognition that is founded in dialogical commmunities." (p. 231)
>
> (Smith, 1988, p. 22)

We need recourse to "dialogical communities" because, as Smith (1988) asserts the attempt to resolve differences due to different interpretations of knowledge claims and from different processes from which these interpretations are derived, "must be undertaken by engaging in rational discourse or dialogue" (p. 22). The learning package in the form of correspondence materials, TV programs, or what have you, should not be expected to stand on its own.

Other authors from different points of view also warn against the oversimplification of ". . .the complex transactional nature of educational encounters" (Brookfield, 1988, p. 20). Brookfield, for example, has characterized the educational process as:

> . . . a bargaining and negotiating process, through which the wishes, desires, interests, perceived needs and outright demands of the chief players (learners, teachers, administrators) interact in a transactional manner. Educational encounters, in my view, are much more accurately perceived as psycho-social dramas than as either wholly self-directed or wholly other-directed endeavors. Endemic to drama is spontaneity, serendipity and happenstance, all within the structure provided by the script. (p. 20)

Larsen (1986) describes the matter from a somewhat different perspective maintaining that ". . . education is a matter of human development that must never be reduced to mere instruction" (p. 335). He goes on to state that:

> . . . education contains something more than mere instruction, namely situations directed against the transformational processes. These are situations such as discussion, dialogue and explanation, which can contribute to the induction of personal knowledge in the learner. This means that more than ever before the educational process should not be seen in isolation, but should be related to the everyday life of the learner to establish the necessary autobiographical references which turn information into personal knowledge. (p. 334)

Bringing about "situations directed against the transformational processes" is a matter of bringing together the teacher and student through the process of communication. Teaching is not simply passing on content as if it were dogmatic truth. Content may represent important knowledge of society but not unquestioned truth. Teaching must be concerned with the critical analysis of beliefs, norms, and accepted knowledge and understandings. Teaching must also encourage the development of new perspectives based upon the integration of students' existing knowledge with newly acquired knowledge. Finally, the student must validate this emerging knowledge through collaborative and sustained interaction with a teacher and other students. This is the critical thinking cycle so crucial to the educational process. As McPeck (1981) claims, critical thinking is not a frill to be added to education—it must ". . . command a place in any institution committed to the pursuit of education because critical thinking is a necessary condition of it" (p. 37).

LEARNING AND EDUCATION

Considerable confusion has resulted in discussions of distance education because of a failure to distinguish clearly between "learning" and "education." Not all learning situations are educational. Little (1980) in a discussion of adult learning and education uses learning as the overarching construct and differentiates between learning in the natural societal setting (which may be both fortuitous and intentional) and "learning" in a formal instructional setting (which may be both directed by self or by others). While much useful learning occurs in the natural societal setting, it can be inefficient and indeterminate whereas "learning" in an instructional setting is deliberately systematic and, therefore, educational in the usual understanding of that term. Clearly there is an important difference about learning in these two situations. What makes the difference between learning and education is the presence and functional role of a teacher.

For our purposes we will use "learning" as a generic term to refer to all of what we come to know, consciously and unconsciously, by whatever means. A part of that will have come to us through education, that process which is characterized by the interaction of a teacher and a student. Through this interaction, the private knowledge possessed by the student (which is essentially all of what the student has come to know through his or her learning experience) is converted to public knowledge, open for inspection by other minds. In the educational process, specific provision is made for the public review of the student's private knowledge through the intercession of a person who is recognized as a "knower" in the particular field of interest—that is by providing a teacher.

At one level, the interaction between teacher and student is a checking of the student's mastery of a body of factual knowledge and the definitional understanding associated with these facts. In all instances students bring to the educational encounter knowledge obtained from other educational experiences and "private" knowledge derived from learning experienced as one lives one's life. To the extent that a student's factual base or definitional understanding is deficient, then a role of the teacher is to supply such declarative information (Anderson, 1983) either directly by "telling" or indirectly by guiding the student to appropriate reference material.

In the fullest sense of education, the interaction between teacher and ⚹ ℛ.𝒞. student is a dialectical exchange which is a "negotiation of meaning" (Rowntree, 1975) around the concepts and relationships of interest (or to use the language of Larsen and Anderson, the interaction between teacher and student induces procedural and elaborated knowledge in the learner). In the very best of these dialectical (or dialogic) exchanges teachers may also experience a validation and elaboration of their own knowledge because of insights either generated by their efforts to include in learning situations "activities devoted to the transformation of information into knowledge" (Larsen, 1986, p. 334) or by students doing for teachers what teachers attempt to do for students. To the extent that distance education denies the importance of the dialogic/dialectical exchange, it runs the risk of diminishing the educational experience or even invalidating it.

Distance education must and will increasingly become seen as education at a distance. Education and distance (between teacher and student, implied) are concomitant features but it is clear in practice that we are attempting to provide educational opportunities for students who just happen to be physically separated from a teacher. Definitions of distance education have typically reversed this emphasis and are preoccupied with the distance feature. It is not surprising, then, that in this context there is an implied equivalence between the technological media used to contend with distance education and the term itself (and the concept it represents). Viewing distance education from the perspective of the technological media used to achieve it obscures the fact that in all instances the goal is education.

As we stated previously, the most important feature for characterizing distance education is not its morphology, but how communication between teacher and student is facilitated. Because the teacher and student are physically separated, distance education must rely on technology to mediate the communication process. However, while considerable attention has been given to the use of technological media, less attention has been paid to the nature of the communication process and the role of technologies in supporting it. We contend that understanding the concept of communication is of central importance to understanding this role. Therefore, a deeper understanding and appreciation of the substantive and qualitative differences among various modes of communication is important. Also, because we are concerned with the modes of communication in an educational situation, an analysis and development of the often vague concept of communication is necessary.

THE NATURE OF THE COMMUNICATION PROCESS

Classically, the communication process was conceived as a sender transmitting a message to a receiver. However, this simplistic model has subsequently been enhanced by a consideration of additional elements such as the medium of communication and the effect that the message has on *both* the partners in the communication relationship. Schramm (1983) states that "communication is now seen as a transaction in which both parties are active" (p. 14). He goes on to say that while both partners need not necessarily be equally active, it "is illuminating to think of communication as a relationship built around the exchange of information" (Schramm, 1983, p. 15).

While Schramm's description of communication goes a long way to ensure there is meaningful interaction, the question remains as to what exactly is meant by "both partners are active." If the message simply stimulates the receiver in isolation, then we must classify this as one-way communication. Books, lectures, and broadcast messages are examples of one-way communication where the receiver accepts the message and is expected to act in a particular manner. However, as Rowntree (1975) declares, this is essentially manipulative. On the other hand, we will consider communication to be two-way if it is facilitative and "allows room for the negotiation of meaning and the prospect of mutual learning through dialogue and discussion" (Rowntree, 1975, p. 284). The distinguishing feature of two-way communication then is that each participant in the relationship is both a sender and receiver and true messages go in both directions.

The response to a message is often referred to as feedback. Since the term is used frequently in educational situations we'll briefly explore what it means. A message in either direction will be referred to as feedback if it goes beyond simply confirming that the message has been received. Store and Armstrong (1981) provide a description of the characteristics of good feedback in an educational setting. They state that good feedback must be explanatory rather than judgmental. From the teacher's perspective this means more than just confirming whether the student is right or wrong. In two-way communication the feedback will explain why the student is correct or "the process by which a student can achieve the correct answer" (Store & Armstrong, 1981, p. 151). In essence, there will be some degree of sustained interaction between the participants that will constitute the "negotiation of meaning and the prospect of mutual learning through dialogue and discussion."

COMMUNICATION AND DISTANCE EDUCATION THEORY

We have stated that two-way communication is an essential process in any educational relationship. And as Salomon (1981) claims, "One could hardly argue with the assertion that education depends on acts of communication." The importance of this process is magnified in distance education because teacher and student are apart. In distance education we are seldom afforded the luxury of direct face-to-face communication; communication usually must be mediated technologically. Because of the importance of communication in distance education it is necessary to understand the impact of mediated forms of communication on the educational process.

Wedemeyer (1981) has provided a model that explicitly identifies the crucial role of the communication mode in distance education. This model identifies four essential elements in distance education and the interactions among them. The importance of the communication process is graphically highlighted in this model and the relative independence and control afforded the learner is apparent.

Figure 1: Wedemeyer's Model

Wedemeyer (1981) states that, "Teaching and learning can safely and effectively be carried on with no loss of interaction, through various communication means, even though teacher and learner are separated in space and time" (p. 37). While it is true that distance education is "safe and effective," the contention that it can "be carried on with no loss of interaction" needs to be examined more closely. There are clearly qualitative and even substantive differences resulting from the various modes of communication. If we are to design more effective and efficient educational relationships we must have a broader appreciation of the communicative process and of the technology needed to support the interaction between teacher and student appropriately.

Many distance education theorists accept the central role that communication plays in teaching and learning at a distance. For example, Keegan (1986) states that one of the essential characteristics of distance education is "the provision of two-way communication so that the student may benefit from or even initiate dialogue" (p. 49). In correspondence study, this provision of two-way communication is a special problem. Traditionally, it has simply consisted of written exchanges sent through the mail. Consequently, two-way communication in correspondence study is delayed, infrequent, and often inadequate for many purposes unless it is enhanced with other communication modes. In this regard, Holmberg (1984) has stated that, "The great weakness of distance education has in most cases been the slowness of the communication processes caused by the correspondence method dominating this kind of education" (p. 50).

Holmberg (1985) has described distance education "as a mediated form of guided didactic conversation" (p. 3). Conversation or interaction occurs through written and telephone conversation which he refers to as real conversation. He also suggests that internal conversation is brought about through the interaction with the print matter itself. Wedemeyer's model also seems to suggest this relationship by connecting "Learner" and "Content" with a two-way arrow. (Although it's not entirely clear, it seems that this relationship is also implied by the two-way arrow joining teacher and content). A question that arises is whether this internal conversation, referred to as simulated didactic conversation, could be considered sufficient in itself to support the educational process. Nilsen (1986), in his attempt to define correspondence education, states that simulated didactic conversation in correspondence education teaches no more than a good textbook and is without the "outer circle" characteristic of two-way conversation (p. 24). Holmberg's argument for this being a true form of conversation is also considered "dubious" by Keegan (1986). The fact that simulated guided didactic conversation is not true two-way communication is put to rest by Holmberg himself when he refers to it as "one-way traffic." He states that, "indirectly conversation is brought about by the presentation of study matter as this one-way traffic causes students to discuss the contents with themselves" (Holmberg, 1985, p. 3).

One distance educator who has recognized the importance of supporting the educational process beyond simply presenting information is Sewart. Sewart (1981) has suggested that distance educators might begin to divide the complex interactive process of teaching "into the subject matter and advice/support" (p. 10). Advice and support are dependent upon extensive use of two-way communication. It deals with how students fit the new knowledge into existing conceptual frameworks and life styles. Learning, in Sewart's scheme, is based largely upon interaction.

Another theorist, Moore, has described distance education from the perspective of the learner's independence. Distance education is much broader than correspondence study. In Moore's description of distance education considerable attention is given to the method of communication due to the independence of the learner as a result of being separated in time and space from the teacher. He states that the "effectiveness of distance education is determined by a complex interaction of variables which include learner variables, teacher variables, subject variables, and communication variables" (Moore, 1986, p. 11). Communication variables are largely concerned with dialogue and structure and ". . . in combination lie at the heart of all educational transactions" (Moore, 1986, p. 11). It is the extent to which two-way communication is provided that reflects the responsiveness to the learner's needs and therefore the quality of the educational program. Again we see the central and essential nature of the communication process as reflected by theorists who view distance education from either a narrow or broad perspective.

AN ALTERNATIVE TO THE WEDEMEYER MODEL

Given the case made to this point, we would like to offer our own model of the educational process, expressed in terms of communication between teacher and student. The traditional, face-to-face mode of communication can be characterized broadly as: the teacher verbally transmits information which is received by the student, and this is followed by discussion (i.e., meaning is negotiated). We can represent this as:

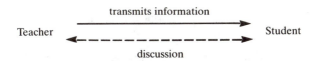

Figure 2: The Traditional Educational Transaction

One could argue that this is a false distinction because in a true educational experience, the student could also transmit information, and in fact information is also transmitted both ways in the discussion. This is true, but representing the exchange in this way will help elaborate the representation of the exchange in distance education.

The natural inclination in distance education practice will be to seek technologies that support the replication of this face-to-face interaction (but at a distance, of course). In this case, the model would be the same as above, but all exchanges are mediated by a black box of technology interjected between the teacher and learner. However, once again the approach of seeking a technology casts the problem as one of "media selection" rather than "media utilization" (Kearsley, 1984). While such an approach will be satisfactory if appropriate two-way communication technologies are readily available (for example, teleconferencing), it may encourage the selection of a less than optimal technology and a philosophy of making do (as, for example, would be the case if television were regarded as the medium for instruction). One consequence may then be a predisposition to believe that education results when, in fact, by our definition it wouldn't. Another consequence is that the possibility of using a mix of technologies to assure two-way communication may be overlooked. However, if one regards the problem as ensuring that the communication loop between teacher and student is closed, then the issue simply becomes: what configuration of technology may be used to do this.

In the absence of two-way communication technologies, the educational exchange in distance education takes on the following form:

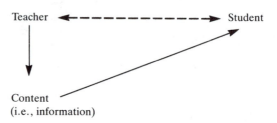

Figure 3: The Educational Relationship in Distance Education

The teacher generates information which is captured by some enduring medium (such as print, audiotape, laser disc). The medium carries the content forward to the student who may then be regarded as having received information. The "negotiation of meaning" required to close the communication loop is an activity separate from the transmission of information and frequently is supported by a medium different from that used to distribute the content. The negotiation clearly will be mediated by a technological medium, and depending on the technology, exchanges may be either delayed or direct. It is, however, the communication loop that unifies the concepts of distance (with its focus on technological structures) and education (with its focus on instructional activities).

CONCLUSION

We have argued that in distance education we must go beyond the current preoccupation with technology and begin to better understand the process of "education at a distance." We maintain that the most important aspect of the educational transaction is what happens after the student has been presented with the content. In distance education this creates a special problem. With teacher and student being separated, greater effort is required to understand the communication process so vital to support the learning activity. Therefore, we believe that the communication process is an essential and defining component of the educational transaction. As Perry (1986) states, "You can indulge in distance learning by reading books. But if you indulge in distance education you are necessarily involved in a two-way communication process. There must be a feedback mechanism for education to happen" (p. 1).

Larson (1985) advises us that "If our understanding of communication interactions do not keep pace with advances in technology, we will be unprepared to put that technology to use in a productive way" (p. 19). The challenge, then, is how to use technology to support the two-way communication between teacher and learner. While all forms of the communication process have a place in the educational transaction, "the system overall must allow for and indeed encourage two-way communication between teacher and the student as regularly as possible so that ambiguities, misconceptions and frustrations are minimized" (Smith, 1979, p. ix).

REFERENCES

Anderson, J. R. (1983). *The architecture of cognition*. Harvard University Press, Cambridge, MA.

Brookfield, S. (1988). Conceptual, methodological and practical ambiguities in self-directed learning. In H. B. Long (Ed.), *Self-directed learning: Application and theory*. University of Georgia; Athens, Georgia.

Daniel, J. S. and C. Marquis (1979). Interaction and independence: Getting the mixture right. *Teaching at a Distance*, 15, 29–44.

Dewey, J. (1917). *Democracy and education.* New York: The Macmillan Company.

Garrison, D. R. and Baynton, M. (1987). Beyond independence in distance education: The concept of control. *The American Journal of Distance Education,* 1(3), 3–15.

Garrison, D. R. and Shale, D. (1987). Mapping the boundaries of distance education: Problems in defining the field. *The American Journal of Distance Education,* 1(1), 7–13.

Harris, D. (1987). *Openness and Closure in Distance Education.* London: The Falmer Press.

Holmberg, B. (1986). *Growth and structure of distance education.* London: Croom Helm.

Holmberg, B. (1985). *Status and trends of distance education.* Sweden: Lector Publishing.

Holmberg, B. (1984). On the educational potentials of information technology with special regard to distance education. *I.C.D.E. Bulletin,* 6, 49–53.

Kearsley, G. (1984). *Training and technology.* Reading, Massachusetts: Addison-Wesley Publishing Company.

Keegan, D. (1986). *The Foundations of Distance Education.* London: Croom Helm.

Larsen, S. (1986). Information can be transmitted but knowledge must be induced. *Programmed Learning and Educational Technology,* 23(4), 331–337.

Larson, R. (1985). What communication theories can teach the designer of computer-based training. *Educational Technology,* 25(97), 16–19.

Lawson, K. (1974). Learning situations or educational situations? *Adult Education* (NIAE), 47(2), 88–92.

Little, D. (1980). Adult learning and education: A concept analysis. In P. Cunningham (Ed.), *Yearbook of adult and continuing education, 1979–80.* Chicago: Marquis Academic Media.

Ljosa, E. (1988). The boundaries of distance education. *Journal of Distance Education,* III(1), Spring, 85–88.

McPeck, J. E. (1981). *Critical thinking and education.* Oxford: Martin Robertson.

Moore, M. (1986). Self-directed learning and distance education. *Journal of Distance Education.* 1(1) 7–24.

Nilsen, E. (1986). On the definition of correspondence education. *Epistolo-didaktika,* 1, 3–30.

Perry, W. (1986). The evolution of distance education. Paper presented at the Distance Education Conference, Vancouver, B.C.

Rowntree, D. (1975). Two styles of communication and their implications for learning. In Baggaly, J., Jamieson, H., and Marchant, H. (Eds.) *Aspects of Educational Technology: Volume VIII, Communication and Learning.* London: Pitman Publishing.

Salomon, G. (1981). *Communication and education: Social and psychological interactions.* London: Sage Publications.

Schramm, W. (1983). The unique perspective of communication: A retrospective view. *Journal of Communication,* 33(3), 6–17.

Sewart, D. (1981). Distance teaching: A contradiction in terms? *Teaching at a Distance,* 19, 8–18.

Smith, K. C. (1979). *External studies at New England: A silver jubilee review 1955–1979.* Armidale, New South Wales: The University of New England.

Smith, J. K. (1988). The evaluator/researcher as person vs. the person as evaluator/researcher. *Educational Researcher,* March.

Store, R. and Armstrong, J. (1981). Personalizing feedback between teacher and student in the context of a particular model of distance teaching. *British Journal of Educational Technology,* 2(12), 140–157.

Wedemeyer, C. (1981). *Learning at the backdoor: Reflections on non-traditional learning in the lifespan.* Madison: University of Wisconsin Press.

CHAPTER 4

COMMUNICATIONS TECHNOLOGY

D. Randy Garrison

The capability of technology to facilitate and enhance communication is transforming the educational enterprise. As a result of new and emerging communications technology, conventional educational systems are being challenged by innovative decentralized systems that reach out to students to offer education at the time, place, and pace appropriate for each learner.

The importance of technology in distance education is due to its capability and potential to mediate communication between teacher and student. As has been emphasized in previous chapters, education is a collaborative experience which necessitates mediation by others as well as recognition and validation of learning. However, technology must go beyond simply providing access to learning through a one-way transfer of prepackaged information. The real power of technology is to reach out to learners, and through two-way mediated communication support their educational efforts by expediting the transformation of information into knowledge.

Until the beginning of the 1970s, print and the mail system were invariably the technology of distance education, generally referred to as correspondence study. Correspondence study has been described as the first generation of distance education technology (Garrison, 1988). It is characterized by the mass production of materials and seen by Peters (1983) as an industrialized form of education. The difficulty with correspondence study is, however, the infrequent, inefficient, and awkward form of communication between teacher and student. The obvious need to mitigate the limitations of pure correspondence study lead to the adoption of mass media; in particular, broadcast television.

The first serious move into the technological age of distance education was made by the British Open University which opened in 1971. Holmberg (1986) has stated that the Open University marked a new era of distance education. This era was distinguished by the extensive use of broadcast media—especially television. The British Open University rep-

41

resented, according to Daniel (1977), the continuance of "a century-old tradition of correspondence education, and raising the methods of independent study to a new level of sophistication by integrating the electronic media with its print-led courses" (p. 130). It signified the beginning of the use of new and emerging communications technology to expand the opportunity to learn at a distance and began to recognize the need for enhanced support through additional channels of communication.

There has, however, been another significant shift in our thinking regarding the design and implementation of education at a distance. It has resulted from the emergence of technologies which can extend the influence of the educator and benefit the learner through immediate and sustained *two-way* communication. As a result, there has been an interactive and individualized (not independent) approach to education at a distance, representing a significant distinction between broadcast media and interactive technologies. Advances in telecommunications and computer technologies have begun a process of "de-massifying" (a term coined by Paulo Freire) media. Distance educators are beginning to understand the educational transaction and the use of technology and media to personalize and individualize programs and information directed toward specific target audiences. Unique and powerful communication systems are being designed by distance educators through the integration of old and new media and technology.

UNDERSTANDING TECHNOLOGY

The means to understanding technology for educational purposes is to focus upon its communication capabilities. Communication capabilities can provide access as well as facilitate ongoing interactive support of the educational transaction. The printed word does provide extensive access to information but it is severely limited with regard to the negotiation of meaning and validation of knowledge through sustained dialogue. Emerging technologies viewed through a communication perspective reveal a means of accelerating negotiation and dialogue between (among) teacher and student(s) at a distance. To understand the role and importance of technology in distance education is to appreciate its capabilities in assisting mediated communication between teacher and student.

Larsen (1985) believes that if "our understanding of communication interactions do not keep pace with advances in technology, we will be unprepared to put that technology to use in a productive way" (p. 19). For this reason we classify and discuss emerging distance education technologies from the perspective of their communication capabilities. While it is difficult to separate various communications technology in practice, it is important to provide some parsimonious ordering if we are to appreciate the range of characteristics and capabilities of developing communications technology. Garrison (1989) has described and discussed in detail distance education technologies from the perspective of their communication characteristics. Communications technology is separated into two-way and one-way communication capabilities. Two-way communications technology consists of three generations or distinct types —print (correspondence), telecommunications (teleconferencing), and computer based. It is the second and third generations, along with a variety of other one-way communications media that we describe as emerging technologies and that are to be discussed in greater detail.

TELECONFERENCING

The two-way communications loop using print materials depends on mail systems. For many educational methods and techniques this is simply an unacceptable means of communication between teacher and student. As noted earlier, a new era in distance education came about as a result of the British Open University using telecommunications technology (notably television and radio) to play a significant role in distance delivery of education. However, telecommunications were used largely to package and distribute information in the form of images to students and did not take advantage of its real power to implement two-way communication between individuals (i.e., telephone tutorials), and in particular, among teacher and students at a distance (i.e., teleconferencing).

The use of telecommunications in distance education marks a new generation in designing the educational transaction. However, contrary to popular belief, the leading telecommunications technology is *not* broadcast television. The quintessential technology of this second generation is teleconferencing. The reason is its ability to conduct immediate two-way communication among several individuals. Teleconferencing conjoins two or more groups through telecommunications technology. Telecommunication channels may be simply telephone and cable transmission, or more recent innovations such as satellite and fiber optics.

The two primary kinds of teleconferencing are audio and video. From an instructional viewpoint both types are capable of providing group interaction. The dynamics of the group are often essential to explore and convey aspects of certain curricula. It also provides opportunities for social support and informal evaluative comparisons amongst the students regarding their academic progress.

There is one other critical advantage of a group method of distance education. This concerns the inherent resistance in many post-secondary educational institutions to accept methodological innovations. Daniel (1984) states that distance education "must be aware of departing from the conventional in more than one of the three key areas of curriculum, staff, and methods. . . . The more a system breaks with conventional methods the less respectable it is likely to be" (p. 27). Because group methods of instruction are perhaps easier for traditional educators to relate to and understand, administrators and instructors in traditional institutions are more likely to adopt an innovation that is analogous to the traditional classroom method which emphasizes interactiveness among students and instructor. In this situation curriculum and staff may remain constant while there is only a slight modification of the group method of delivery.

Audio teleconferencing is currently the most prevalent form of teleconferencing in distance education. While audio teleconferencing can be traced to the late 1930s, it was not until the 1970s that extensive use of audio teleconferencing in distance education began (Olgren & Parker, 1983). Audio teleconferencing is particularly appealing due not only to its educational qualities but also to its cost-effectiveness. Hardware costs are relatively inexpensive and may be leased to evaluate this delivery method as a pilot project. Instructors do not require large amounts of time and money to develop a course since curriculum and its delivery is likely to be similar to their traditional method of instruction. Long distance charges are the most serious on-going cost, but if distances are not extreme and centers are kept to a reasonable number, these costs can be affordable. If the number of students is relatively small, in comparison to correspondence study, audio teleconferencing represents a more cost-effective method while providing considerably more educational support and direction.

Video conferencing, on the other hand, is far more complex and costly compared to audio or enhanced audio teleconferencing. As a result, video teleconferencing has not experienced as wide an acceptance as audio teleconferencing. Olgren and Parker (1983) report that only 16 percent of organizations that use video conferencing for educational purposes use full-motion video.

Two-way exchange of video images between two or more sites and three or more individuals can create a technical nightmare. Such a system allows a student to see the teacher and also provides visual images of the students at the remote sites to the teacher. However, the costs and technical problems invariably preclude the adoption of true two-way video conferencing for educational purposes. Most applications of video conferencing make use of one-way video and two-way audio where only the students can see the teacher but the audio is fully interactive.

While visual interaction is advantageous, and in some situations necessary, in the vast majority of distance education applications, full motion video is an unnecessary luxury. Keeping in mind that in most video conferencing situations there is only one-way video transmission, the use of real-time video must be critically assessed for each specific application. A maxim provided by Johnson (1983) says "Any communication is maximized at its simplest effective level" (p. 125). While establishing an effective level of communication for distance education may be difficult, most often it does not include full motion video. More will be said about full motion video (i.e., television) as a medium of educational communication in the ancillary media section of this chapter and as well as a full treatment in Chapter 10.

COMPUTER-BASED TECHNOLOGY

Computer-based learning in conventional education classrooms has made few inroads because of its primary use as an adjunct to traditional methods, and as such, it is seen simply as another added responsibility for the teacher. In distance education, however, technology is an essential component of the transaction and distance educators are generally open to new approaches to provide better access and support for learning at a distance. And in distance education, as in society as a whole, the microprocessor has created much excitement with its potential to access and process information. While the conventional education system appears to have lost its capacity to adapt to technological change, distance educators have in many cases become the true innovators with regard to the educational application of computer-based technological systems. The potential for worthwhile applications of computer-based technology is virtually unlimited in distance education.

Computer-based technology is a unique technological advancement. As such it also offers unique educational possibilities and, therefore, is seen as the third generation of distance education. Although computer assisted learning has been with us since 1959, computer-based distance education is only an emerging development. The uniqueness and significance of this technology is found in its capacity to sustain a high degree of independence and still provide quality learning diagnostics and feedback.

Communication through a computer is of two distinct types with regard to distance education applications. The first type is the *transmitted or on-line mode* where the computer is integrated with telecommunications technology. The second type is the *local or off-line mode.* Together they offer the distance educator an unequalled range of instructional methods and techniques.

Perhaps the most immediately applicable computer-based technology to distance education is the *transmitted mode.* Examples of uses of the transmitted mode for distance education are computer conferencing, electronic mail, accessing electronic data bases, and administrative applications. All of these functions build naturally upon previous technologies such as print and telecommunications. They should not be seen as replacing older technologies but as expanding the range and types of instructional alternatives available to distance educators.

Computer conferencing has many similarities to audio and video teleconferencing. However, since it is based upon the information processing capabilities of computers, it represents a unique form of communication. Messages are organized and stored by the computer and communication is asynchronous and in a graphic form. While such communication is not ideal for many educational purposes, it does have the advantage of conducting group communication over time at the convenience of the participants. In short, group communication is independent of distance and time.

Electronic mail is similar to computer conferencing except that it is an individual to individual method of communication. It has an enormous advantage in distance education in providing individual support and quick turnaround time on assignments. Electronic databases can also be of great advantage to the distance learner in accessing relevant and current information. Finally, administrative functions such as developing course materials and delivering these materials to the learner can provide considerable efficiencies in managing a distance education program.

Using the computer in *local mode* holds great promise for distance education in the future. Computer-based instruction in the local mode is a move away from impersonal mass produced packages of materials to an individualized system under the direct control of the learner. The promise of this technology is seen in the current applications of computer managed learning (CML), computer assisted learning (CAL), and intelligent computer assisted learning (ICAL).

Computer managed learning may be used in the local mode to identify learning resources and evaluate student progress both formatively and summatively. Such guidance and feedback can be of enormous benefit to geographically isolated students. CML in transmitted mode can also be used to communicate student records to the institution as well as offering an educational intervention in the other direction if necessary.

Computer assisted learning is a broad concept covering educational applications such as drill and practice, tutoring, simulating, and problem solving. The characteristics that make these applications of value educationally is their interactive instructional capabilities. The great disadvantage, however, is the lack of relevant and quality courseware. Much greater efforts are required in designing more sophisticated software and courseware. The current excitement in this area is with the application of artificial intelligence techniques to CAL.

Two areas of research in artificial intelligence (AI) of particular relevance to education are expert systems and natural language processing. It is the advances and use of expert systems and to a lesser degree natural language processing that have caught the attention of educators and offer great promise in the future. The combination of AI techniques and CAL results in *intelligent computer assisted learning* (ICAL) systems which "offer a reactive learning environment, where the student is actively engaged with the instructional system and his/her interests and misconceptions drive the tutorial dialogue" (Rambally, 1986, p. 39).

Rambally (1986) has described ICAL as generally consisting of four modules—expert module, tutorial module, student module, and interface module. The expert module contains the subject matter and generates problems for solution. The tutorial module contains the instructional strategies, rules, and processes. The student module is responsible for adjusting instruction to the needs, knowledge, and abilities of the student. And finally, the interface module provides the communication knowledge for the student to interface with the computer using natural language. While progress is being made with ICAL, this field is still in its infancy and no system exists today with each of the components fully developed. However, not withstanding the current limitations of ICAL, its potential access and support capabilities represent a vision capable of significantly advancing education at a distance.

ICAL holds out the promise of an effective tutorial dialogue where the learner is challenged and meaning is negotiated. In this sense interactivity is seen as the involvement of the learner in the educational process. In a discussion of interactivity within the context of computer-based tutoring systems, Morrison (1987) suggests there is a difference between physical interactivity and mental interactivity. In many ways this classification corresponds to internal and external aspects of the educational transaction as well as to confirmatory and explanatory feedback. Morrison (1987) argues that simply responding to multiple choice questions represents largely a physical interactivity at the expense of "really crucial interactivity—that between the user's thoughts and the material to be learned" (p. 135). Mental interactivity is demanded for many higher level learning tasks. Through mental interactivity possibilities of real control over learning are afforded the learner. For computer-based software we must strive for standards which induce greater levels of mental interactivity. The same, however, could be said for all educational methods. The challenge for distance educators is to understand the communication process and its technological possibilities so that we achieve mental (internal) activity; not just physical activity which does little to expand awareness and develop knowledge.

ANCILLARY MEDIA

The discussion to this point has focused upon the three basic communications technology. Clearly there are other existing and emerging communications hardware of enormous value to distance education. The kinds of hardware discussed in this section are referred to as media because of their inability or inadequacy of supporting two-way communication in an educational context. As a result, they are invariably combined with the previously discussed technologies.

One medium deserving special attention is television. *Broadcast television* played an important role in establishing the credibility and prestige that distance education currently enjoys. However, as rich a medium as television is, it remains a one-way communication system. Broadcast television is an efficient method of distributing visual information; but because of its non-interactive nature, it tends to be a passive medium where the educational message is not always clear to the observer. In addition, broadcast television is often inconvenient in terms of the time and place of viewing. To give more control to the learner and allow for greater integration with other course materials, the video cassette is gaining greater acceptance. For these reasons, Moore (1987) states that in the United States he expects "a diminishing role for broadcast television" (p. 43).

The key issue in the use of television or video is how it should be integrated in the instructional design. One of the most exciting educational uses of video images is that of the *laser videodisc*. In terms of computer-based learning, the laser videodisc is perhaps the best example of ancillary media. The videodisc by itself represents a means of storing vast amounts of audio-visual information and accessing it in a second or two. However, when the laser disc is interfaced with a microcomputer the educational potential increases enormously. Fuller (1984), in a discussion of distance education technology states that for "individualized, interactive education there is no competition to the computer/ videodisc" (p. 72). The power and potential of interactive videodisc will provide the foundation and means for quality computer-based distance delivery in an independent and interactive manner.

The most prevalent and useful ancillary media associated with teleconferencing are called audiographic enhancements. *Audiographics* refers "to the transmission of graphics and text information over a narrowband telecommunications channel, such as a telephone line" (Olgren & Parker, 1983, p. 321). The three most frequently used audiographic media are facsimile, slow-scan (freeze-frame) television, and telewriting.

A facsimile system can transmit a hard print or image copy and reproduce it at a remote site. While this system is useful, it does not integrate well into the real-time educational transaction. The second audiographic example is slow-scan television which transmits still video images over a narrow-band channel (e.g., telephone line). This system may be advantageous for specific applications but normally takes 30–40 seconds to transmit an image. Telewriting is the third audiographic device and acts as an electronic overhead projector and blackboard. With some telewriting systems students may interact with the image or create their own. Because of its capabilities, telewriting naturally integrates with teleconference methods.

CONCLUSION

Emerging communications technology is not only changing how distance education is practiced but it is also having profound effects on how we conceptualize the field. We have noted how technology is demassifying educational methods at a distance. It is causing many distance educators to rethink the essence of distance education. The relationship of teacher and students in traditional correspondence study has evolved considerably as a result of emerging communications technology. Concomitantly and equally significant, distance educators are no longer dependent upon one technology or medium.

The major technologies of distance education presented here have been somewhat artificially separated into generations. Although it is useful to distinguish between these technologies for taxonomic purposes, it should be noted that only rarely are they found in practice in their pure form. Invariably the generations build upon each other, and when combined with ancillary media, it becomes difficult to classify the technology as belonging to one generation or the other. Such integration of technologies and media provide a greater range of possibilities and challenge in designing education at a distance. The ultimate purpose of which is to support the educational transaction for the benefit of the learner.

Through the use of communications technology, education is no longer confined within the walls of traditional institutions. Students have the opportunity to study in their homes, community, and workplace while still experiencing a quality learning experience through the guidance and support of qualified teachers. Although communications technology can provide access to education, the real impact of the emerging distance education technologies discussed here is the support of learning by facilitating the two-way communication so necessary in the educational transaction. A quality educational transaction is a collaborative experience between teacher and student, and emerging personal communications technology "will extend the possibilities for humane learning beyond what was possible in the broadcast era" (Daniel, 1984, p. 4).

However, a hardware perspective of technology will not in itself realize significant progress in supporting the educational transaction at a distance. The existence of technology does not ensure adoption, or more importantly, the appropriate application of technology in the support of the educational transaction. Hall (1987) states that, telecommunications may increase access to learning but "such access to knowledge does not in itself produce a learning situation: that state in which the learner is fully active" (p. 47). He goes on to say that we must avoid the illusion of access by stimulating behavior but instead encourage "a posture and practice for learning that is active, alert, serious" (Hall, 1987, p. 48). We must recognize that distance education is dependent upon technological devices, but the effectiveness of the educational transaction is dependent upon the facilitation of communication and the active involvement of the learner. As Howard (1987) suggests, it "may in fact be that a new technology does have the potential for great instructional innovation, but it must be emphasized that it is the innovative instructional applications of these that matter, that is, their *functional value* in instructional terms" (pp. 25–26).

Before concluding this chapter it must be noted that emerging technologies have the potential of widening the gap between the educated and the undereducated. Distance education has been championed as a means of providing equitable access for continuing education regardless of socioeconomic status. If distance education becomes increasingly technologically based, then it will become a privilege of the well-educated who are able to afford the latest technology to access educational programs. One solution to this dilemma may be learning centers where the technology is equally available to all segments of society. The learning center has been promoted as a supportive student-centered approach and alternative to isolated distance learning (Sewart, 1987). The multiplicity of provision offered in a learning center can address the negative bias that new technologies may present to the undereducated.

We believe that it is distance educators who are grasping the significance of communications technology and are becoming the leading innovators in the educational technology field. As such, distance education provides a rich and promising environment for applications of this technology. However, these issues are not the topics here but will be addressed in subsequent chapters on designing programs for distance delivery.

REFERENCES

Daniel, J. S. (1977). The open university concept. *Canadian Journal of Information Science, 2,* 129–138.

Daniel, J. S. (1984). *Media of distance education: Prospects and effectiveness.* Proceedings of the 2nd International Symposium on Media of Distance teaching, Korea Correspondence University.

Fuller, R. (1984). Video discs. In R. W. Gates (Ed.), *The role of technology in distance education* (pp. 67–75). London: Croom-Helm.

Garrison, D. R. (1989). *Understanding distance education: A framework for the future.* London: Routledge.

Hall, J. (1987). Bridging the technology-pedagogy gap. In P. Smith & M. Kelly (Eds.), *Distance education and the mainstream: Convergence in education* (pp. 44–56). London: Croom-Helm.

Holmberg, B. (1986). *Growth and structure of distance education.* London: Croom Helm.

Johnson, J. W. (1983). Anatomy of a teleconference. In E. A. Laser, M. C. J. Elton, & J. W. Johnson (Eds.), *The teleconference handbook: A guide to cost-effective communication* (pp. 125–140). White Plains, N.Y.: Knowledge Industry Publications.

Larsen, R. E. (1985). What communication theories can teach the designer of computer-based training. *Educational Technology, 25*(7), 16–19.

Morrison, D. J. (1987). Interactive learning systems and the learner. In F. Percival, D. Craig, & D. Buglass (Eds.), *Aspects of educational technology Volume XX: Flexible learning systems.* London: Kogan Page.

Moore, M. G. (1987). Distance learning in the United States: The near future. *Distance Education, 8*(1), 38–46.

Olgren, C. H., & Parker, L. A. (1983). *Teleconferencing technology and application.* Dedham, MA: Artech House Inc.

Peters, O. (1983). Distance teaching and industrial production: A comparative interpretation in outline. In D. Sewart, D. Keegan, & B. Holmberg (Eds.), *Distance education: International perspectives* (pp. 95–113). London: Croom Helm.

Rambally, G. K. (1986). The AI approach to CAI. *The Computing Teacher,* April, 39–42.

Sewart, D. (1987). Limitations of the learning package. In M. Thorpe, & D. Grugeon (Eds.), *Open learning for adults* (pp. 31–33). Burnt Hill, U.K.: Longman House.

Willis, N. (1984). Technology: Agent of change. *Media in Education and Development,* June, 74–82.

CHAPTER 5

MEDIA AND INSTRUCTIONAL METHODS

Bill Winn

A few years ago, Richard Clark created a stir in the educational technology community by claiming that there was nothing intrinsic to media that made the slightest difference to how well people learn from mediated instruction (Clark, 1983). Clark's argument was compelling. He demonstrated that studies showing superior performance by students in mediated treatment groups were either methodologically flawed or seriously confounded and thus open to equally viable alternative interpretations. He concluded that it was instructional methods that really made the difference, and urged researchers and practitioners to attend to these rather than to media which merely deliver instruction while remaining neutral to it. Clark has not avoided criticism (Petkovich & Tennyson, 1984), but he has stood by his position (Clark, 1985a, 1985b, 1987) and has persuaded a large number of scholars that he is right.

Media may not affect how well people learn. However, there is no denying that they greatly affect the efficiency with which instruction can be delivered. The storage of still images on videodisk rather than in a slide library increases the efficiency with which they can be used to teach. Interactive teleconferencing is a far more efficient medium for the exchange of ideas than the postal service. Some of these advantages of technology have been confirmed empirically (see, for example, Wager, 1986), and others doubtless will be.

The distance educator faces the task of selecting the most effective instructional methods for teaching and of choosing the most efficient medium for delivery. Normally, the selection of the delivery medium is the last decision that the instructional developer should make (Reiser & Gagne, 1983) because the instructional methods have the greatest impact and must therefore be chosen first. Once methods are chosen, the range of prossibly useful media is restricted to just a few, and the final selection can be easily made usually on the basis of cost-effectiveness. However, the distance educator is in a different position in this regard. Given the need to reach students who are away from the instructor, the

53

use of certain media is usually imposed *a priori,* and often with cost rather than sound pedagogy in mind. Consequently, the distance educator does not have a complete range of instructional methods available, but must select only those that the medium is capable of delivering. For example, in classroom instruction, an instructional developer might decide that socratic tutoring is the best method to use. Assuming that the same content has to be delivered by correspondence, socratic tutoring will be excluded, and the distance educator will have to settle for another less effective method. In distance education, as it is defined in this book, this is less of a problem than it might otherwise be. Adults in distance education courses tend to be highly motivated (Knox, 1977), and motivated students can learn well enough in spite of less than optimal instruction. Yet the trade-offs between instructional methods and the constraints imposed by delivery technologies need constant attention from distance educators.

The purpose of this chapter is to present a fairly broad overview of educational technology while keeping in mind the distinction between delivery media and instructional methods. This will necessitate an examination, later, of how technologies constrain instructional methods and what this means for the design of distance education programs. We begin with an examination of the main advantages that it has been claimed technology can bring to education.

EDUCATIONAL TECHNOLOGY

If we set aside the supposition that the media make a difference to how people learn, we nonetheless find a number of reasonable claims for the advantages of using technology in education. Some time ago, Edling and Paulson (1972) summarized these in three categories which even today capture well a number of ideas about what technology can do. There are technologies that allow us to make information permanent. These include all recording technologies such as audio and videotape, photographic film, optical and magnetic disks, print and paper, microforms, and so on. While these technologies perform a useful archival function, they also allow the recording and replication of superior instruction. It has been claimed that this ultimately can lead to the improvement of education by capturing the best instruction with a view to making it widely available.

Technologies exist that make information easily available. While using technology to record good instruction made subsequent distribution possible, other technologies made access to recorded information even easier.

These include telecommunications that allow access to information over long distances, and information retrieval technologies that allow rapid and random access to stored information. When telecommunications and information retrieval technologies work together, it is possible to access information in databases that are at great distances from the user. When the user is a student, then these technologies can be used in any of a number of ways—as a library to be consulted, for example, or under the control of an instructor as instantaneous information displays that can be used during a lesson like the chalkboard or overhead projector.

Finally, we can use technology to make information different. Here, ③ we are talking about message design as much as we are about technologies. The idea is simply that we can take information and, by varying the the method of presentation, change what it means. We have understood for most of this century how film and video editing can do this. We are now beginning to understand how varying such things as illustrations (Duchastel and Waller, 1979; Goldsmith, 1984), computer screen display (Alessandrini, 1985; Merrill, 1982) and text itself (Duffy and Waller, 1985; Jonassen, 1987) affect how people process information and learn from it. Moreover, interactive video, with the possibility it provides for changing the sequence of images during instruction, offers a potential for implementing a whole new set of instructional techniques.

These three functions of technology—making information permanent, making it accessible, and making it different—are all extremely important for the distance educator, although available delivery technologies may well constrain the extent of their implementation. It is possible to make recorded information available to students either electronically or by mail and courier services. It is possible to tie students at remote sites into any available database. It is possible to present information to students, either live or in support materials in any of a number of formats that have been designed to optimize learning. So while we tend to think first and foremost of telecommunications technologies when we talk about distance education, we must not lose sight of the other advantages technology can bring.

So far we have looked at educational advantages of technology that derive largely from hardware. There is another side to technology that many claim is more important (AECT, 1977; Winn, 1986). This we will refer to as "instructional technology" in contrast to "delivery technology" which we have been discussing so far.

The development of a large number of alternative ways of recording, accessing and altering information offered to educators a large number of alternatives to the traditional techniques of instructing. With this increase in available choices came the need for much more attention to be paid to instructional decision making, planning and management. A new conception of technology crept into education which treated technology as a process of applying knowledge to tasks (AECT, 1972, 1977; Knirk and Gustafson, 1986). The roots of this conception can be traced to Galbraith's definition of technology as the systematic application of knowledge to tasks (1971). The idea of "systematic application" is extremely important, for to succeed it requires what Glaser (1976, 1985), like Dewey before him (Dewey, 1926), has referred to as a "linking science" between instructional theory and practice. According to Glaser (1976), this "linking science" is essentially a science of design. Design can best be thought of as a decision-making process in which the designer selects the best possible method to use given a set of constraints. In the instructional context, this means the identification of the most effective instructional methods given the outcomes instruction is intended to achieve and the conditions under which it is to occur (Glaser, 1976; Reigeluth, 1983).

INSTRUCTIONAL DESIGN

Reigeluth's (1983) suggestion that all instructional theories should contain propositions relating instructional methods to instructional outcomes and conditions provides a useful framework for the distance educator. We need to look more closely at what "conditions," "methods" and "outcomes" are. Our discussion has led us to the point where the centrality of instructional methods to instructional technology is becoming apparent, so we shall begin with these. Let us therefore return for a moment to the ideas of Clark concerning methods with which this chapter began.

Methods make the difference, not media. But what is a method? In his article, Clark (1983) implies that what we often consider to be methods are really media, which do not have an impact on learning. We may talk of the "lecture method," where an instructor makes an oral presentation to a classroom of students. The lecture is really nothing more than a way of delivering information. If a recorded lecture were played back to students who had missed the live lecture, one would not expect any great difference in how much they learned compared to those who had attended the live lecture, even though the apparent "method" is entirely different. On the other hand, the lecturer could present a lecture once with and once without interruptions for questions. Here, although using the "lecture method" in both cases, one might well expect differences in learning to occur.

From this example, it is clear that differences in methods must be described according to cognitive criteria. The lecture which allows students to interrupt and ask questions makes it possible for students to confirm or correct the accuracy of their processing of the presented information in "real time." The information is processed differently and different cognitive skills are brought into play—for example, formulating a useful question rather than accurately transcribing the lecturer's words for later consideration. In an earlier paper, Clark (1982) describes a "method" in just these terms, as a strategy that has a direct impact on ← cognitive processing. This leads to the implication that the instructional designer selects instructional methods on the basis of their known and predictable effects on cognitive processes, and that the theory that underlies educational technology is psychological theory (Winn, 1988).

Now let us turn to instructional outcomes. These are usually considered ← to be the goals and objectives that instruction is intended to help students attain. Instructional designers have developed a number of ways of identifying and classifying instructional outcomes (Bloom, 1956; Gagne, 1984; Merrill, 1983), and each serves well within the context of the design procedures embodied in the particular design theories and models. Traditionally, instructional outcomes have been couched in behavioral terms (Mager, 1962; Dick and Carey, 1985). However, this view poses a problem. Given that methods are concerned with cognitive processes, we can no longer continue to think of instructional outcomes as behaviors. If that were the case, there would be no way of determining whether our methods have been effective. We must therefore think of outcomes not simply as behaviors but in terms of the acquisition of knowledge and cognitive skills. Although Greeno used the term "cognitive objective" over a decade ago (Greeno, 1976), it has taken quite a time for cognitive instructional theories, such as those proposed by Rumelhart and Norman (1981) and Anderson (1983), to emerge. The serious attention of instructional technologists to the role of cognitive theories in instructional design has likewise been quite recent (Winn, 1988; Bonner, 1988).

The upshot has been that instructional technologists are beginning to question a number of the assumptions about human learning that have traditionally underpinned instructional design and technology. For the distance educator, there are important ramifications. First, by and large distance education courses are more carefully and extensively designed than courses delivered face-to-face, meaning that they take longer to prepare. The need to identify cognitive processes rather than observable behaviors as learning outcomes makes this preparation even more difficult and burdensome, though techniques for doing this, such as Scandura's (1983) "Structural Analysis," are proven and available.

Second, it has been shown that the kind of learning that methods derived from cognitive theory rely on (for instance, the alteration and creation of knowledge schemata through their interaction with new information [Rumelhart and Norman, 1981]; the compilation of procedural knowledge from declarative knowledge [Anderson, 1983]; and problem solving generally) can often best be taught by means of a tutorial dialogue. As is well known, this instructional method is difficult to implement in distance education except where more costly systems are available to support a high degree of interaction.

Instructional conditions are those things over which the instructional designer usually has no control. The most obvious examples are characteristics of the students, such as aptitude and learning styles, that can usually be changed only in exceptional circumstances. A great deal of research has been directed at defining relationships between student characteristics, instructional methods and the outcomes of instruction, and has been summarized by Cronbach and Snow (1977) and Snow, Federico and Montague (1980). Because of the difficulty of studying and describing all possible permutations of student characteristics and instructional methods, and because other factors appear to be more influential than student characteristics in determining the outcomes of instruction, the value of this research for instructional decision making has been questioned (Merrill, 1975).

One instructional "condition" whose importance no one doubts is how much the student already knows about what is to be taught (Tobias, 1976). Indeed, Gagne's theory of learning (1985) and the instructional theory that is based on it (Gagne, Briggs and Wager, 1988) deals extensively with prerequisite knowledge of content and mastery of prerequisite intellectual skills. Learning hierarchies are constructed so as to identify the knowledge and skills that underlie everything the student has to learn. Thus knowledge and skills that the student must possess before beginning the instruction is determined as well as the knowledge and skills that the student must acquire, sequentially, during the instruction. It is safe to say that, while not all instructional theories or design models put as much emphasis on prerequisite knowledge and skills as Gagne's theory, all deal with this matter to some extent.

Another important condition of instruction concerns the motivation of the students. Almost alone amongst instructional design theorists, Keller has paid particular attention to this issue (Keller, 1983, 1987). Beyond that, of increasing interest to instructional technologists is attribution theory (Schunk, 1984). Simply put, it is claimed that people's expectations of how well they will learn something is an important determinant of how well they will actually do. People's expectations are known to vary from content area to content area—math is a "hard" subject—(Harvey, 1984), and also from medium to medium—television is "easy" and text is "hard"—(Salomon, 1984). The instructional designer must consider the kinds of attributions students are likely to make to the instruction that they will receive.

The distance educator needs to attend to all of these conditions of instruction. It is particularly important to determine what knowledge and skills the students possess upon which the instruction can safely build. In face-to-face instruction, it is much easier for the teacher to determine whether the instruction is above the students' heads than it is when the students cannot be seen or cannot interact easily. The distance educator confronts a different set of motivational problems than the classroom teacher. By and large, adults attending distance education classes are well motivated. However, particularly if an innovative technology is being used, students may not be all that confident that the system can teach them well. The problem is one of attribution or "self-efficacy" rather than motivation. Distance educators can also attend to learning styles and aptitudes of students. Students may simply not believe that they can learn at a distance. However, there is probably little likelihood that the distance educator will have the opportunity to design instruction to suit individual differences. The instructional systems tend to be too rigid, and the opportunities to diagnose student aptitudes and styles and monitor the appropriateness of instruction for those characteristics are just too infrequent to warrant the energy that these activities require.

INSTRUCTIONAL METHODS FOR DISTANCE EDUCATION

The techniques instructional designers use for selecting instructional methods for given conditions and outcomes are described elsewhere in this book. It is sufficient to say here that they involve techniques for analyzing the needs to be met and the tasks to be performed, and for analyzing the conditions that prevail, particularly the characteristics of the students. They also involve techniques for field-testing instruction so that problems can be diagnosed and corrected before instruction is implemented. Also, a number of instructional design models prescribe which methods to use for various permutations of outcomes and conditions. The Gagne-Briggs instructional theory (Aronson and Briggs, 1983), for example, presents instructional methods in a chart in which five types of instructional outcome are crossed with nine "events" that must occur if instruction is to succeed. Other theories, perhaps the majority, are far less prescriptive and seem to devote most of their attention to analysis and evaluation. Regardless of which theory the distance educator subscribes to, the hardest task is the selection of appropriate instructional methods, and most theories are not particularly helpful in this regard.

The selection of methods requires a comprehensive knowledge of how people learn and how best to instruct them, a sound understanding of the factors that influence learning (some of which were discussed in the preceding section), and a good mix of experience and common sense. For the distance educator, it also requires a comprehensive repertoire of methods that are effective in spite of the constraints that result from the *a priori* imposition of delivery technologies. (This is not to say that the media are always givens. Britain's Open University took a number of years to decide upon the delivery systems, and the decisions were made frequently for pedagogical reasons. However, distance educators do not often enjoy that situation.) We now look at some of the methods such a repertoire might contain.

Our discussion proceeds from assumptions derived from cognitive theories of learning. First, new knowledge and skills are always learned in terms of what students already know. This is a fundamental tenet of cognitive learning theory (Gagne, 1985) and reaches its clearest expression in schema theories of learning and memory (Anderson, 1977; Rumelhart & Norman, 1981). Second, it is rare that the intended outcome of instruction is simply to acquire facts. Declarative knowledge is sometimes considered the starting point from which a variety of cognitive skills are built. Landa (1983), for example, describes how instruction should teach operations that act on knowledge in order to transform it into more powerful skills and abilities. Anderson (1983) describes a process in which declarative knowledge is transformed into procedural knowledge that can be applied more generally to classes of problems.

Third, the more mental elaboration information undergoes, the better it will be integrated into long-term memory and learned (Reder, 1982). That is to say, the more the student works to try to make sense of it, the better it will be understood and remembered.

Fourth, students need guidance about how to study. It is insufficient simply to present information to students. Except for those who have the ability to monitor their own performance and to select learning strategies once they have found out how well they are doing (see Brown, Campione and Day, 1981), students will not learn well unless they are given directions as to what learning strategy to employ (Rigney, 1978).

Fifth, students often benefit if they have a certain measure of control over the instruction they receive. This can be looked at in two ways. On the "micro" level, students working on their own do better if they are allowed to choose such things as how much practice they do for given instructional items and where they go once they have completed a particular task, provided that they receive advice from the instructional system that is based on a knowledge of their progress. On a "macro" level, adult students like to have a say in what they are to study and are better motivated if they take part in the instructional planning process.

It is probably evident that each of these points requires that students be able to interact extensively with the instruction or instructor. This, of course, is the hardest thing to achieve in distance education because the student is removed from the instructor in space and often in time as well. The previous comments therefore have as their basis the general notion that students should interact with the instructor as much as possible during the individual lessons. Students should also be provided with materials and exercises to work with between lessons that facilitate such things as the assimilation of new knowledge into existing schemata, the compilation of procedural knowledge from facts and the deployment of effective learning strategies.

MEDIA FOR THESE METHODS

We have in a sense come full circle. Our discussion has led us from the idea of media as delivery systems, to instructional technology and design, to an examination of cognitive approaches and to the identification of five areas of instruction where distance educators face particular difficulties as they choose appropriate methods. In each case, the fact that students cannot easily and immediately interact with an instructor places constraints on the distance educator that would not normally affect the selection of instructional methods. We conclude this chapter by discussing media systems that permit maximum interaction and therefore minimize these constraints.

The technologies available to us allow two qualitatively different types of interaction to take place. The first involves attempts to imitate the live classroom as closely as possible. Here we find the development of interactive video and audio telecommunications systems (e.g., teleconferencing) which bring the student into contact with the instructor in classes at regular intervals. The second involves technologies that provide the opportunity for students to interact with the materials, rather than with an instructor, in their own time and usually in their own home. These technologies include varieties of programmed instruction and interactive computer-assisted instruction where a student may log into a mainframe located at a central site, or may work on a home computer using software provided for the course. (A third set of technologies, which send information one way to students at a distance are equally important, but are not discussed here because they are not interactive.)

When distance educators develop systems that aim to provide all of the advantages of classroom instruction that students at a distance often have to do without, a number of requirements for the hardware and the instructor must be met. Obviously, the hardware must allow for immediate and spontaneous interaction. This requires at a minimum two-way audio and easy-to-use microphones that are provided with typical telephone teleconferencing systems. The addition of one-way graphic and perhaps video capability is often necessary so that prepared images can be used to illustrate presentations. Failing that, supporting graphic materials can be sent to students ahead of time for reference during a lesson. Overhead transparencies or slides can be shown at local study centers by proctors, although this usually proves to be cumbersome and prone to error. The addition of two-way video is something of a luxury, but nonetheless allows an even closer approximation to the classroom. With the media in place, the responsibility for effective interaction falls squarely on the shoulders of the instructor. It is much harder for even experienced instructors to achieve interaction using, say, a teleconferencing system than it is in a classroom. There are many reasons for this. Eye contact is not possible, so it is harder to determine which students are not following the presentation. (Sometimes instructors do not even know which students are actually present!) Also, even with the simplest systems, some extra effort is always required for a student to ask or answer a question, or to seek a clarification. The instructor must deliberately encourage interaction and not wait for it to happen on its own. Questions to ask of students, and when to ask them, must be planned ahead of time. Changes of pace, from presentation to discussion to exercises, must be made and planned for. A new sense of pacing must be developed so that the instructor allows more time between asking a question and expecting a response. Instructors must get used to directing questions to particular students, in turn. In sort, distance education that uses live instructors requires the development of entirely new teaching techniques.

Systems that require students to study largely, or exclusively, on their own employ different technologies and must rely on different techniques to bring about interaction. First, the technologies must be interactive. Programmed texts and computers are not. Broadcast radio and television are not. The responsibility for interaction lies with the designer of the instructional materials rather than with an instructor, but the same general principles apply. The students must have the opportunity to respond frequently to questions asked by the system and to apply their new knowledge and skills in exercises and problem-solving activities. They must also have the same access to guidance that students have who are in contact with an instructor. The materials must come with all manner of help that the student can call on as needed. Computer software must therefore have extensive "help screens." Self-instructional texts must have appendices containing reference material and guidance on how to study. What is more, the materials themselves must be carefully designed to embody the best in instructional methods. Particular care should be given to screen or text layout, the use of illustrations, charts and graphs, the level of the language and directions on how to perform exercises. The materials must be capable of teaching effectively with minimum recourse to a live instructor or advisor.

It is encouraging that many of the better-known distance education systems meet these criteria. It is also clear that people getting into the business for the first time might well think that distance education is not really any different from education in classrooms, and therefore requires little beyond the installation of the hardware. This chapter has made the case that nothing could be further from the truth. The media simply deliver instruction; they do not make it good or bad. The instruction can only be good if the designer, and the instructor when there is one, select the most effective instructional methods on the basis of what is known about how people learn. Most of the best methods inevitably require interaction between the student and the instructor or the materials. The technologies that are typically used in distance education can constrain this essential interaction unless the designers and instructors take particular pains to make sure that it occurs. It is that effort, which is not normally needed in as great a measure in classroom instruction, that makes distance education so different. If distance educators fail to realize this and fail to make the necessary effort, they will not be successful.

REFERENCES

Alesandrini, K. L. (1985, April). Visual formatting in computer-based screen design. Paper presented at the meeting of the American Educational Research Association, Chicago.

Anderson, J. R. (1983). *The architecture of cognition.* Cambridge, MA: Harvard University Press.

Anderson, R. C. (1977). The notion of schemata and the educational enterprise.

In R. C. Anderson, R. J. Spiro, & W. E. Montague (Eds.), *Schooling and the acquisition of knowledge,* (pp. 415–431). Hillsdale, NJ: Lawrence Erlbaum Associates.

Association for Educational Communication and Technology (1972). Educational Technology: A statement of definition. *Audiovisual Instruction, 17(8),* 36–43.

Association for Educational Communication and Technology (1977). *Educational Technology: Definition and a glossary of terms.* Washington DC: Association for Educational Communication and Technology.

Aronson, D. T., & Briggs, L. J. (1983). Contributions of Gagne and Briggs to a prescriptive model of instruction. In C. M. Reigeluth (Ed.), *Instructional design theories and models,* (pp. 75–100). Hillsdale, NJ: Larence Erlbaum Associates.

Bloom, B. S. (1956). *Taxonomy of educational objectives. Handbook I: Cognitive domain.* New York: David McKay.

Bonner, J. (1988). Implications of cognitive theory for instructional design: Revisited. *Educational Communication and Technology Journal, 35,* 3–14.

Brown, A. L., Campione, J. C., & Day, J. D. (1981). Learning to learn: On training students to learn from texts. *Educational Researcher, 10 (2),* 14–21.

Clark, R. E. (1982, April). Instructional methods: Operational definitions and criteria attributes. Presented at the meeting of the American Educational Research Association, New York.

Clark, R. E. (1983). Reconsidering research on learning from media. *Review of Educational Research, 53,* 445–460.

Clark, R. E. (1985a). Clark's reply. *Educational Communication and Technology Journal, 32,* 238–241.

Clark, R. E. (1985b). Evidence for confounding in computer-based instruction studies: Analyzing the meta-analyses. *Educational Communication and Technology Journal, 33,* 249–262.

Clark, R. E. (1987, February). Which technology for what purpose? Presented at an invited symposium at the meeting of the Association for Educational Communication and Technology, Atlanta, GA.

Cronbach, L. J., & Snow, R. E. (1977). *Aptitudes and instructional methods.* New York: Irvington.

Dewey, J. (1926). *The sources of a science of education.* New York: Liveright.

Dick, W., & Carey, L. (1985). *The systematic design of instruction,* (2nd edition). Glenview, IL: Scott, Foresman.

Duchastel, P., & Waller, R. (1979). Pictorial illustration in instructional texts. *Educational Technology, 19 (11),* 20–25.

Duffy, T., & Waller, R. (1985). *Designing usable texts.* New York: Academic Press.

Edling, J. V., & Paulson, C. F. (1972). Understanding instructional media. In National Specific Media Institutes, *Contributions of behavioral science to instructional technology, Volume 2: The cognitive domain,* pp. 161–199. Washington DC: Gryphon House.

Gagne, R. M. (1984). Learning outcomes and their effects. Useful categories of human performance. *American Psychologist, 39,* 377–385.

Gagne, R. M. (1985). *The conditions of learning,* (4th edition). New York: Holt, Rinehart and Winston.

Gagne, R. M., Briggs, L. J., & Wager, W. (1988). *Principles of instructional design,* (3rd edition). New York: Holt, Rinehart and Winston.

Galbraith, J. K. (1971). *The new industrial state.* New York: The American Library.

Goldsmith, E. (1984). *Research into illustration.* Cambridge: Cambridge University Press.

Greeno, J. G. (1976). Cognitive objectives of instruction: Theory of knowledge for solving problems and answering questions. In D. Klahr (Ed.), *Cognition and instruction.* Hillsdale, NJ: Lawrence Erlbaum Associates.

Glaser, R. (1976a). Components of a psychology of instruction: Towards a science of design. *Review of Educational Research, 46,* 1–24.

Glaser, R. (1976b). Cognitive psychology and instructional design. In D. Klahr (Ed.), *Cognition and instruction,* (pp. 303–315). Hillsdale, NJ: Lawrence Erlbaum Associates.

Glaser, R. (1985). Learning and instruction: A letter from a time capsule. In S. F. Chipman, J. W. Segal & R. Glaser (Eds.), *Thinking and learning skills, Volume 2: Research and open questions,* (pp. 609–618). Hillsdale, NJ: Lawrence Erlbaum Associates.

Harvey, T. J. (1984). Gender differences in subject preference and perception of subject importance among third year secondary school pupils in single-sex and mixed comprehensive schools. *Educational Studies. 10,* 243–253.

Jonassen, D. (1987). *The technology of text, Volumes 1 and 2.* Englewood Cliffs, NJ: Educational Technology Publications.

Keller, J. M. (1983). Motivational design of instruction. In C. M. Reigeluth (Ed.), *Instructional design theories and models,* (pp. 383–434). Hillsdale, NJ: Lawrence Erlbaum Associates.

Keller, J. M. (1987). Motivational design. In R. McAleese & D. Unwin (Eds.). *Encyclopedia of educational media, communications and technology.* Westport, CT: Greenwood Press.

Knirk, F. G., & Gustafson, K. L. (1986). *Instructional technology: A systematic approach to education.* New York: Holt, Rinehart and Winston.

Knox, A. (1977). *Adult development and learning.* San Francisco, CA: Jossey Bass.

Landa, L. N. (1983). The algo-heuristic theory of instruction. In C. M. Reigeluth (Ed.), *Instructional design theories and models.* Hillsdale, NJ: Lawrence Erlbaum Associates.

Mager, R. F. (1962). *Preparing instructional objectives.* Palo Alto, CA: Fearon Publishing.

Merrill, M. D. (1975). Learner control: Beyond aptitude-treatment interactions. *AV Communication review, 23,* 217–226.

Merrill, M. D. (1983). Component display theory. In C. M. Reigeluth (Ed.),

Instructional design theories and models, (pp. 279–333). Hillsdale, NJ: Lawrence Erlbaum Associates.

Merrill, P. (1982). Displaying text on microcomputers. In D. Jonassen (Ed.), *The technology of text, Volume 1,* (pp. 401–414). Englewood Cliffs, NJ: Educational Technology Publications.

Petkovich, M. D., & Tennyson, R. D. (1985). Clark's "Learning from media": A critique. *Educational Communication and Technology Journal, 32,* 233–241.

Reder, L. M. (1982). Elaborations: When do they help and when do they hurt? *Text, 2,* 211–224.

Reigeluth, C. M. (1983). Instructional design: What is it and why is it? In C. M. Reigeluth (Ed.), *Instructional design theories and models,* (pp. 3–36). Hillsdale, NJ: Lawrence Erlbaum Associates.

Reiser, R. A., & Gagne, R. M. (1983). *Selecting media for instruction.* Englewood Cliffs, NJ: Educational Technology Publications.

Rigney, J. W. (1978). Learning strategies: A theoretical perspective. In H. F. O'Neil (Ed.), *Learning Strategies.* (pp. 165–205). New York: Academic Press.

Rumelhart, D. E., & Norman, D. A. (1981). Analogical processes in learning. In J. R. Anderson (Ed.), *Cognitive skills and their acquisition,* (pp. 335–359). Hillsdale, NJ: Lawrence Erlbaum Associates.

Salomon, G. (1984). Television is "easy" and print is "hard": The differential investment of mental effort in learning as a function of perceptions and attributions. *Journal of Educational Psychology, 76,* 647–658.

Scandura, J. M. (1983). Instructional strategies based on the structural learning theory. In C. M. Reigeluth (Ed.). *Instructional design theories and models,* (pp. 213–246). Hillsdale, NJ: Lawrence Erlbaum Associates.

Schunk, D. H. (1984). Self-efficacy perspective on achievement behavior. *Educational Psychologist, 19,* 48–58.

Snow, R. E., Federico, P. A., & Montague, W. E. (1980). *Aptitude, learning and instruction.* Hillsdale, NJ: Lawrence Erlbaum Associates.

Wager, W. (1986). Comparative analysis of television tutorial and CAI for the teaching of typing skills to radio-teletypewriter operators. *Educational Communication and Technology Journal, 33,* 97–104.

Winn, W. D. (1986). Trends and future directions in educational technology research from a North American perspective. *Programmed Learning and Educational Technology, 23,* 346–355.

Winn, W. D. (1988, February). The theoretical foundations of educational technology and future directions for the field. Presented at the meeting of the Association for Educational Communications and Technology, New Orleans, LA.

CHAPTER 6

INSTRUCTIONAL DEVELOPMENT CONCERNS

Erv Schieman

The appearance of technology adaptable to instruction has been both a blessing and a curse to educators. It is a blessing in the sense that as the technology becomes more sophisticated and available at relatively low costs, the greater are the options open to the educator who strives to make instruction interesting and varied, and of course, meaningful.

On the other hand, advances in the instructional technologies have also tended to be a problem for many educators, including those in the distance education field. With the capability of providing interactive instruction to be carried out at a distance has come the problem of providing careful and comprehensive planning to ensure that instructional goals are being met and the further problem of how to employ the technology to exploit its interactive potential. The focus of this chapter will be the identification of concerns to the distance educator in the development of effective and efficient instruction.

SOME GENERAL GUIDELINES FOR DEVELOPING INSTRUCTION

Whether performed by the developer, the subject matter specialist or another instructor in the same area, a rationale should be in place before embarking on the lengthy and often time consuming procedure of development. What is required is a systematic, organized method for dealing with the many aspects of the procedure in question. Basically the result would be something similar to the following:

* a reason for designing the program, course or series of lessons which would incorporate the terminal instructional goals.
* a strategy or map including enabling objectives (possibly organized

in a comprehensive way following the plan of Bloom, 1956). Included here would be some listing of skills, knowledge and abilities expected of the learners.

* the development of an instructional strategy which would describe the units of instruction, their intended learning outcomes, the teaching strategies to be employed and the development and/or selection of teaching materials (see, for example, Dick and Carey, 1985, Chapter 8).

* an evaluation plan, certainly of a formative type and possibly including summative evaluation algorithms. The intent must be to evaluate not only the performance of the learners but also the check and balance of the course itself, with a view to improving the method of instruction.

* the reexamination of the entry behaviors of the learners must be an on-going activity. The impetus for the continual reexamination comes from the analysis of the results of the learners and possibly from the changes which may be apparent in the rationale or need for the course or program.

These considerations provide a broad framework within which instruction may be developed. Though no detailed description of the instructional development process will be given here, (for example, see Bass and Dills, 1984), a heuristic approach for creators of distance education courses and programs is provided. There is some grain of truth in the notion that there are as many instructional development models as there are instructional designers (Andrews and Goodson, 1980). However, there are elements of all models which appear to be common (for example, see Dick, 1981), and they can be summarized in the following general way:

* state the purpose of the course or program
* outline the content to be taught
* decide on a time allocation for the units or elements
* decide on the appropriateness of the plan for the intended audience
* list the skills and the procedures to be developed
* produce the instructional materials
* devise evaluation procedures

While the order of the above plan may and probably will vary from developer to developer the essence of the process is there. The "how" of the process is the creative endeavor brought to the development by the individual educator/developer. With these prominent ideas in mind, the developer can begin to conceptualize how the new or modified design for a course or program can begin to take shape.

Instruction must go beyond the phase where students simply are expected to collect factual/definitional kinds of information and extend to levels where the learners' thought processes lead to in-depth learning. Instructional development should be extended to a consideration of conversational knowledge (which includes the memorization of terms, recognition of relationships between terms, classification of unique uses of terms and also the application of the new terms in unique situations). As well, the teaching of procedural knowledge would also be a goal of certain categories of instruction and training. In this instance the designer/educator would develop a strategy for dealing with the abilities and skills needed to progress through some formal procedure to arrive at a way to solve a problem. The analysis of this procedural matrix makes it possible to identify enabling or subordinate skills needed to complete a task and to assess the outcomes of instruction (Dick & Carey, 1985). The third class of knowledge often included in course development exercises is known as causal knowledge. Extending beyond recall and recognition, and even beyond the expert use of procedures to learn tasks, causal knowledge involves using two or more principles to reach a prediction or diagnosis of a problem. This higher level of learning is usually associated with mastery learning and is probably the level most instructors the world over attempt to achieve. Developing instruction for the teaching of skills at the mastery level involves a consideration which is concomitantly both a benefit and a problem for instructional developers. Namely, how to manage the time factor. In mastery learning, time becomes the variable on which learner achievement depends. The underlying belief is that through variation in the time allowed for instruction, all learners can realize success at a prescribed level of achievement (Cronbach and Snow, 1977). Recognizing the problems and limitations of trying to develop mastery level learning, developers are still able to employ a systematic strategy to design effective courses and programs. This may be especially true for such diverse skills as keyboarding, video editing and blood typing, to name only a few. Generally, any skill subject that requires standardized learning materials would be suitable for this type of learning.

Given this broad context for planning course or program development, there are several additional conditions that can affect development which will be examined. It is intended that these be general to alert the reader to their existence but not necessarily to provide working procedures for integration into an actual design.

MAJOR DESIGN ISSUES

For whom is the course or program intended?

At every stage of the planning, production and evaluation phases, it is imperative that the recipients of the instruction be the central focus. The developer needs to consider their entry level skills and knowledge, their personal and professional needs, their level of maturity or development (necessary to know so that the developer can employ appropriate levels of concept complexity) and finally their interests.

Should the characteristics of the potential audience be unfamiliar, then one of several strategies may be called for. For example, the developer could choose to approach the course instructor/content specialist to determine where a likely beginning or entry point might be. This individual's knowledge of the audience, assuming he/she has experience with this group, would serve to identify the parameters of the learners' backgrounds and possibly suggest appropriate beginning concepts, vocabulary, etc. and also identify the range of concepts appropriate for the course or program. Another suggestion which would assist the developer would be to actually observe similar courses with similar learners. This experience combined with the other kinds of information would put the developer in a more confident position regarding the nature of the intended audience. No doubt other techniques such as pretesting and experience profiles would be useful as well (see, for example, Dick and Carey, 1985).

A great deal has been written regarding the modes of instruction best suited for learners of different age groups (see, for example, Travers, 1977) and the employment of various strategies for effective learning (see, for example, Weinstein and Mayer, 1985; Posner and Rudnitsky, 1986). However, there is some question whether the research regarding how learning takes place and the design of effective instruction can be generalized to learners of all ages and especially to adults. Little attention has been directed by educators to the possible differences in the way adults and young people learn. The assumption often is that little difference exists in the belief that well designed learning materials are equally effective with most audiences.

Sequencing strategies

An aspect of course and program development often given too little consideration is the matter of the logical and appropriate organization of critical concepts in order to best facilitate learning of new material. Although the suggestions below are shown as discrete entities, they can be viewed as combinations which would best suit the particular instruction being developed.

Certain educational psychologists have argued that course content is not as important to course organization as is the way learners learn (Gagne, 1970; Ausubel, 1964). Therefore, in examples employing this type of perspective, one would find material sequenced on the basis of interest and information processing. For example, in teaching writing, letter recognition and letter formation would precede the actual teaching of writing words and sentences.

New information can also be sequenced to match the learner's needs regarding the social, career or personal contexts or organization. These three areas are useful especially for the grouping of the intended learning outcomes into units and ultimately for the grouping of the units. In each of the clustered units, content can be sequenced to reflect procedures for solving particular problems. With content that has a procedural basis, the sequence would reflect the order in which the steps would ordinarily be utilized. As well, the design may follow a sequence of steps ranging from those judged to be the most important to those of lesser importance. The important steps would be those that the learner would have to deal with most frequently.

The developer might carry out the organization of the content around major ideas. How the major ideas relate to each other would be an additional concern and decisions would have to be made regarding which would be the most important of the major ideas. The notion of developing concept maps reflects this type of planning so that at a glance the developer can "conceptualize" the ingredients of the units, their organization and sequencing. From this, decisions can be made regarding the possible strategies of teaching deductively or inductively. This approach can be useful when the developer must decide which fundamental aspects of a discipline are needed to form the major idea. Learners then can learn "structures" of content rather than all the details necessary to formulate major ideas and their interrelationships.

A developer could view the learner having the ability to generate, discover and verify knowledge given certain tools with which to work. The process can follow several different patterns. From one perspective the process of discovery can be thought of as a matter of generalizing from many instances of occurrence of a phenomenon. The instruction would then include examples of the generalization to promote the actual discovery of the generalization. Also, when instruction is organized to test conjectures, hypotheses are elicited from the process with the learner then required to collect data to substantiate the claims. This perspective often results in instructional strategies where results of research are taught before the learner is required to form ideas, questions or hypotheses about the optimal solution.

A sequencing strategy commonly found in textbooks, journals and periodical articles is to show empirical relationships between events, people and objects as they exist. This is juxtaposed with sequences where there is obvious consistency between the method used for organizing units. History books and articles often are sequenced from this perspective. Instruction developed from this perspective is both common and logical and used extensively by educators the world over.

Motivation for learning

For those developers/educators who have been associated with public school, freshmen college and advanced college level learners, it seems clear that adult learners attitudinally bring much more to the experience than do young learners. What appears to be most obvious is that older learners not only can more clearly define their needs but also are often highly motivated to succeed. Instructional developers should capitalize on this in the process of designing effective learning materials. In many cases, the motivation arises because the course may be required by a governmental or professional accreditation agency. Here the incentive for additional remuneration and/or promotion may well be sufficient to ensure successful performance. Building in motivational techniques may also be less of a problem with those learners who have high levels (and enjoy the challenge) of achievement no matter what the content or the instruction might be. Also, the situation where the learners will be required to possess new skills and abilities in order to perform well as their jobs change, can also be a powerful motivating factor. However, most educators have encountered situations where the motivations must be designed into the learning/instructional strategy. This would seem to be especially pertinent to developers of distance education courses where many of the usual strategies in the repertoire of the face-to-face classroom instructor are not available when the learners are remote.

Though often neglected or totally ignored as an instructional design issue (Carroll, 1963), motivation is included in the concept of aptitude (Cronbach and Snow, 1976) or reinforcement/feedback (Skinner, 1968) and is more often treated as an essential element of design models (Reigeluth & Merrill, 1979). However, guidelines and procedures for the actual facilitation of motivation were lacking until Keller (1979,

1987) identified and operationalized his strategy. Therefore, the instructional developer who is otherwise charged with the task of dealing with certain memory and learning problems of adults can take heart in the thought that often high levels of motivation are present in this group of learners.

Interactivity in instruction

The concept of interactive instruction has come to imply situations where the learner is a highly active participant in the instructional event. The learner makes decisions and addresses the consequences of those decisions. Interactivity implies a flexibility of approach so that learners' needs and capabilities are considered. Jonassen (1985), for example, describes interactive lessons as those which have the capability of having learners overtly responding to technology-based information. The system in turn provides feedback to guide the learner in any further participation.

The concept of interactivity is a complex one. A traditional view of interactive instruction would typically have the interactions serve as a checking mechanism where the learner is asked a question about the content and is then presented with a response of some type, usually in a branching method. However, though this is a most important role of interactions, it usually is limited to this one aspect. In more sophisticated systems, questions can be used by the learner in an information-gathering way to locate needed and possibly crucial information. The learner should have the means to command the system to locate this information.

Relying on relatively easy to use search strategies as a means for retrieving information with on-line systems or optical disc storage systems such as CD-ROM, learners are able to access, in an interactive way, necessary information. In all cases, some type of information retrieval capability must be incorporated into the system. The best method, however, is still being determined. Certainly menus and maps make the process much simpler.

The new technologies of instruction raise yet another issue for the instructional developer. The great versatility of a medium, such as video, allows for feedback methods of a nontraditional form. Feedback need not be limited to the written or spoken word. With interactive video, for example, computer generated graphics are an obvious possibility with their many forms such as bolding, color, flashing words, boxes around wordings, underlining, etc. These interactive systems can also be designed to allow learners to check their knowledge of a subject, provide novelty and attention-getting strategies emphasizing and reinforcing important concepts, directing attention, modeling behavior and others. The point is that developers have these attributes available to enhance the instruction they are producing.

Interactive approaches are markedly different from traditional pedagogies where the learners respond to the teacher's methods. Certainly for adult learners this philosophy, if adopted, can release them from a situation of dependence to one of individual initiative. The advantages of interactive strategies include the following points: they encourage learners to be more self-directed; they are problem-centered in their approach to learning; and most important, they address crucial social needs, especially for adult learners.

The question which arises as a result of considering the various forms or levels of interactivity is whether it is possible with well designed alternative instructional strategies to achieve high performance outcomes regardless of the technology being used. Can appropriate lessons of equal effectiveness be produced with many strategies? Clark (1983) has argued that this is entirely possible, since according to his research the delivery system was incidental to the effectively designed instruction. Therefore, if one were to focus attention on the organization of information so that it would be relevant to the individual learner's cognitive processing capabilities, rather than the technology of instruction, then the developer of instruction can attend to the attributes of various media, in order to employ those which best facilitate learning. Gagne, Wager and Rojas (1981) addressed this very concern by attempting to apply the "events of instruction" (Gagne and Briggs, 1979) to the design of CBI tutorials. Examination of each of the five generic instructional phases (orientation, presentation, sequence, encoding and retrieval) revealed that when the approach or perspective included the best way to orient learners to content, for example, several alternatives became evident. No one best technology or strategy was identified. The problem is therefore not defined technologically but is characterized from a learning and processing perspective.

CONCLUSION

Learning at a distance presents a new set of problems for instructors, learners and certainly for the developers of instructional systems. The literature in the field of distance education indicates that variables which influence learning outcomes can be and are usually significantly altered for the remote learner, regardless of age of the learner, course content and choice of instructional delivery system. There are factors peculiar to distance education which are not influences in face-to-face instructional situations. Obvious factors such as the absence of visual contact (unless of course the instruction system includes two-way video teleconferencing) between instructor and learner, eliminates communication cues that normally accompany instructor explanations or learner understandings. Such alterations to the standard classroom environment may cause problems for novice distance education instructors in managing the instructional process.

A process of careful instructional design can, in part, overcome many of the types of problems just described. There are a number of considerations which may influence the effectiveness of distance education. The physical arrangements can be a factor as can the availability of trained site monitors or local teaching assistants. The selection and availability of interactive modes of instruction, including those which are technology-based can make the process a positive learning experience. Teaching roles and styles are also considerations for the distance education developer. The traditional roles of instructors must change to accommodate the attributes and potential of the communications technologies.

When the developer of distance education programs can choose from a repertoire of technologies, the main considerations to be addressed are (1) its delivery characteristics, (2) its presentational characteristics, and (3) its control characteristics. Clearly, the more closely the final choice matches the learner's needs, the better are the chances that it will be effective. The point must be made that if the learner is ultimately to benefit from increased use of distance education technologies, the rationale for adding new technologies must be a pedagogic one rather than a technological one. It is becoming more evident that technology has and is creating increased opportunities for delivering instruction to wide audiences. Technology has also increased the possibilities for learning where only motivation and financial resources are boundaries. For all of these potentials to be realized, however, there must be an awareness by developers and distance educators alike of the need to plan and design the learning materials in an organized and systematic way where as many learning and learner variables as possible are considered.

REFERENCES

Andrews, D. H., & Goodson, L. A. (1980). A comparative analysis of models of instructional design. *Journal of Instructional Development*, 3, 4, 2–16.

Ausubel, D. P. (1964). Some psychological aspects of the structure of knowledge. In S. Elam (Ed.), *Education and structure of knowledge* (pp. 220–262). Chicago: Rand McNally.

Bass, R. K. & Dills, C. R. (1984). *Instructional development: the state of the art, II.* Dubuque, Iowa: Kendall/Hunt.

Bloom, B. S. et al. (1956). *Taxonomy of educational objectives: the classification of educational goals. Handbook 1: cognitive domain.* New York: David McKay.

Carroll, J. B. (1963). A model of school learning. *Teachers College Record, 64,* 723–733.

Clark, R. E. (1983). Reconsidering research on learning from media. *Review of Educational Research, 53,* 445–460.

Cronbach, L. J., & Snow, R. F. (1977). *Aptitudes and instructional methods.* New York: Irvington.

Dick, W. (1981). Instructional design models: Future trends and issues. *Educational Technology, 21,* 7, 29–32.

Dick, W., & Carey, L. (1985). *The systematic design of instruction,* (2nd edition). Glenview, Illinois: Scott Foresman.

Gagne, R. M. (1970). *The conditions of learning,* (2nd edition). New York: Holt, Rinehart and Winston.

Gagne, R. M., & Briggs, L. J. (1979). *Principles of instructional design.* New York: Holt, Rinehart, and Winston.

Gagne, R. M., Wager, W. W., & Rojas, A. (1981). Planning and authoring computer assisted instructional lessons. *Educational Technology, 21,* 17–21.

Jonassen, D. H. (1985). Interactive lesson design: A taxonomy. *Educational Technology, 25,* 6, 7–17.

Keller, J. M. (1979). Motivation and instructional design: A theoretical perspective. *Journal of Instructional Development, 2,* 4, 26–34.

Keller, J. M. (1987). Development and use of the ARC5 model of motivation design. *Journal of Instructional Development, 10,* 3, 2–14.

Posner, G. J., & Rudnitsky, A. N. (1986). *Course design: a guide to curriculum development for teachers,* (3rd edition). White Plains, NY.: Longman Inc.

Reigeluth, C., & Merrill, M. D. (1979). Classes of instructional variables. *Educational Technology,* March, 5–24.

Skinner, B. F. (1968) *The technologies of teaching.* New York: Appleton-Century-Crofts.

Travers, R. M. (1977). *Essentials of learning,* (4th edition). New York: Macmillan.

Weinstein, C., & Mayer, R. (1985). The teaching of learning strategies. In M. C. Wittrock (Ed.), *Handbook of research on teaching,* (3rd edition) (pp. 315–327). New York: Macmillan.

CHAPTER 7

COURSE CREATION ISSUES IN DISTANCE EDUCATION

Mavis Kelly

Distance education is now recognized throughout the world as a viable alternative to campus-based education. In addition to those institutions which teach only at a distance, many others are exploring the option of offering courses in this way, both to increase access to education and to meet the needs of learners who are already in the workforce. In some institutions, techniques of distance education replace or supplement face-to-face lectures under the rubric of resource-based education, while in others courses are offered to groups of learners in locations remote from the main institution. There are clear advantages in adopting these modes of education in terms of widening access to education, fostering a more independent approach to learning, and providing a more economical use of human resources for teaching.

The transition from classroom-based teaching to distance education does, however, require some reorientation on the part of teachers, learners and administrators. New skills need to be acquired by all who participate in terms of planning, course delivery and teaching and learning via the range of technologies that are now available for communication.

This chapter provides an overview of what is involved in planning and preparing a course to be taught by distance education. Some of the issues to be confronted will be familiar to teachers and administrators accustomed to a system of education based primarily on face-to-face tuition. Others will be new issues, arising from the methods of communication available for use in distance education, and, in many cases, from the population of learners who often choose to study in this way.

Basically I will address three topics which are essential to understanding the creation of courses within distance education:

1. Planning issues
2. Course preparation issues and
3. Ongoing support systems for learners

Throughout the discussion, I will not attempt to specify what a distance education delivery system should consist of or how it should function, but rather will present some options currently available, along with the issues that should be examined when these options are considered.

PLANNING ISSUES

The decision to enter into distance education needs to be taken with sufficient regard for planning issues. These issues imply an appreciation of:

1. To what extent existing models of distance education are applicable
2. What kind of infrastructure must be developed to support distance education in an institution
3. What implications for teaching strategies arise from proposed course or program
4. How the targeted student population for the course will affect the design of teaching strategies

Existing Models of Distance Education

In considering how they might develop and manage the task of distance education, many institutions look to the examples provided by others. This needs to be a critical evaluation, taking into account the goals and assumptions underlying existing models. It is important, for instance, to appreciate that though large institutions which teach only at a distance have provided the dominant model for the conduct of distance education for nearly two decades, many other approaches have existed for several years.

In order to be cost-effective, institutions like the British Open University and others which teach only by distance education, rely on detailed and costly preparation of self-instructional resource materials using a range of media, together with enrolment of very large numbers of students in relatively few courses. Students gain access to the British Open University on the basis of open entry and are supported in their study by an extensive network of regional centers throughout Britain and group meetings at summer schools. Creation of resource materials for learning is the limit of teachers' responsibility towards learners, who have no opportunities for ongoing communication with these teachers. Academic support and counselling is the responsibility of other staff employed by the institution as tutors and counsellors. Another prominent feature of the Open University's mode of operation is role diversification, whereby teaching materials are prepared by a team which may consist of a number of academics, educational technologists, instructional designers, editors, audiovisual specialists, computer-assisted learning specialists, and so on. All participate in decision making during course creation and have a shared responsibility for the final outcome.

Systems based on this model can work well and greatly increase access to education, while at the same time containing costs. The drawback is that "distance education" has often been defined in terms of these systems and the assumptions that underlie them, thus inhibiting the development of alternative systems or a full appreciation of existing systems which may be equally viable and cost effective.

I do not anticipate that the model provided by large single-purpose institutions will necessarily be appropriate, for example, in institutions which wish to offer a wide range of courses with relatively few enrolments; in institutions which have quite different entry criteria and populations of learners; in institutions which intend to integrate their on- and off-campus teaching. Each case presents a different context and requires the development of a unique system for distance education.

At the other extreme we might cite cases where institutional philosophy dictates that teachers not only create teaching materials but also assume responsibility for ongoing support for learners. In these cases there is usually also a minimal amount of role diversification. The emphasis is shifted away from production of packages of self-instructional resource materials towards development of a system which relies on regular communication between teachers and learners and among learners themselves: by occasional face-to-face meetings, audio or computer conferences, or electronic mail, for example. Such systems imply a more restricted pattern of access, and do place limits on learners in terms of schedules for teletutorials or other group meetings, but they also offer a regular source of ongoing support in the form of tuition and instruction, vocational advice and personal counselling as well as providing opportunities for one-to-one communication. For a given population of learners the restrictions imposed may be wholly appropriate and acceptable, given the advantages offered.

One basic issue that all institutions face is how to widen access to education, while at the same time providing a delivery system which includes necessary resources as well as an appropriate level of ongoing support. Also the cost of maintaining the system must be contained.

The answers will not necessarily be found by emulating the mode of operation of other institutions, though an examination of existing models will highlight some of the issues to be considered. Overall the important criteria for any distance education system are not whether it conforms strictly to a particular model but whether it is embedded in an institutional framework or infrastructure which allows participants to make informed choices about teaching and learning strategies and administrative procedures and which facilitates communication between participants in the educational process.

Developing a Suitable Infrastructure

What do we mean by an infrastructure for distance education? Basically we refer to the human and physical means needed to locate or develop resources for learning and to carry out ongoing support functions. We also refer to the establishment of systems for storing, accessing and handling information and resource materials and of communication systems to facilitate one-and two-way communication between teachers and learners and among learners.

Regardless of the teaching-learning model that is adopted by an institution, distance education will always be mediated to some extent by nonteaching support staff and by the structures and functions of the institution. Even when teachers assume sole responsibility for course delivery, these processes are only possible where capabilities exist to produce or store resource materials in sufficient quantities and where teachers and learners can communicate, for example, by audio-teleconferencing, electronic mail delivery, postal delivery, one-to-one telephone calls and the like. Moreover these facilities must be available at appropriate times and at reasonable cost. For these reasons the infrastructure that exists in an institution to serve distance education, or which could be adapted to this end, is of crucial importance to individual teachers as well as to the operation of a distance education program as a whole.

The following list will give some idea of the types of teaching and service units, which when integrated into a functioning whole, would form an infrastructure for distance education. This list is not prescriptive but does serve to delineate the range of services that could contribute to a distance education infrastructure.

* Academic teaching units. It is possible to develop a distance education system which does not employ teachers on site, for example by employing outside consultants or by relying heavily on resource materials developed by other institutions, supported by part-time

tutors. However, many institutions prefer a system with a pool of academic teachers available to develop resource materials and communicate with learners. Where the institution already teaches in the face-to-face mode, such a pool of expertise will already exist, though it may, on occasions, need to be supplemented by external teaching staff.

* Educational service unit. Input from professional advisers, experienced in distance education, curriculum design, instructional design, media, communications technology, or adult learning, can provide a valuable input to the development of a distance education course, in particular to the kinds of teaching strategies which will be adopted.

* Production unit. This unit would include staff responsible for word processing or desk top publishing, audio and video cassette making and copying, and printing. As well it will be their responsibility to ensure that appropriate schedules are developed and maintained for production and dispatch of resource materials. Where a substantial number of people are involved in bringing a course to fruition, this unit may also assume responsibility for project management.

* Student services unit. This unit would usually handle administrative enquiries from students, enrolments and enrolment variations, receipt and dispatch of assignments, examination arrangements, academic and personal counselling, organization of tutorials, group meetings, visits by teachers to regional centers and so on.

* Technical services unit. This unit is essential to ensure that all equipment is kept in a good state of repair and would also provide advice on the purchase of new equipment including computer hardware and telecommunications equipment.

* Mailing/Dispatch unit. Where resource materials are to be made available to learners on a regular basis, they need to be dispatched efficiently, have records kept, stock reordered and queries handled.

* Budget/Accounts office. Central to the whole operation is an accounting office familiar with the costs incurred in distance education, which can allocate resources to course creation and engage in planning.

* Postal library. In many institutions a postal library service is an invaluable asset to both learners who may reside some distance from the institutions and teachers who wish to ensure that all students have good access to books and other resource materials. The library may also perform other functions such as on-line database searches, advice to students on choice of learning resources for particular projects and so on.

In some institutions, existing units may be used to carry out some of the functions implied above, but this is only an effective way to proceed if the work flow that can be handled coincides with the schedules of the distance education operation. Part of the work may be contracted out but, once again, only if schedules can be adhered to.

Regardless of the kind of infrastructure that is developed, distance education will invariably cut across established teaching and administrative procedures to some extent. For instance, a portion of the work of course creation should occur well in advance of the teaching sessions, both in terms of planning and preparation of resource materials, in order to provide learners with a comprehensive overview of the course at the beginning of the teaching session. This in turn has implications for course approval procedures which need to be effected earlier than is usually the case in conventional teaching institutions. If a package of resource materials using a variety of media is planned, then additional time must be allocated to this task well in advance. Usually the more complex a distance education operation, the more lead time will be required for the production of materials and to ensure that the appropriate teaching and other staff are available when this preparation is in progress. Moreover, a distance education system can only be developed effectively if sufficient funding is available. Resource allocation typical of on-campus teaching institutions usually fails to take account of the different types of activities which are associated with distance education and of the economies of scale which can be realized under certain conditions: for instance, where a heavy initial investment in preparation of resource materials is justified by large course enrolments and by using the same resource materials over several teaching sessions.

Course-related Issues

In many institutions only a limited subset of services will be available for course creation and ongoing communication with learners and this will influence the choice of media for presenting teaching materials as well as opportunities for contact between teachers and learners. Thus print and audiocassettes are still the most commonly used for learning resource materials in distance education even though particular courses would benefit greatly from an expanded range of media. Ongoing support is often by post or telephone or at residential sessions which may or may not be compulsory.

Both cost factors and conventional views of distance education contribute to the availability of services and resources for course creation. The burden of innovation is often placed on individual teachers who wish to create a distance education course with a range of media and who wish to offer alternative support to learners, having considered fully the course which they are preparing to offer.

If one were in a position to plan without the restrictions imposed by existing structures, then full consideration would have to be given to the content and objectives of the course and to the level at which it will be offered.

Course Content and Objectives

Whether a distance education course is based primarily on self-instructional resource materials or conducted primarily by regular inter-active sessions such as teleconference, it is desirable to outline the main features of the course: its aims and objectives, topics to be covered and assessment requirements, well in advance of the teaching session. This outline enables distance learners without frequent formal or informal contact with teachers and peers to understand the course in overview and to plan to meet the course requirements.

If asked to describe a course, teachers accustomed to face-to-face teaching will frequently produce a table of contents and possibly some information about its credit value and assessment weighting. In a sense this approach is realistic, considering that in the on-campus situation many aspects of the course are taken for granted by students and teachers alike and there are easy opportunities to supply extra information and to change direction if required.

When planning a distance education course, however, a contents list has limited value. It will indicate what areas of knowledge are to be covered though not necessarily how topics are related to each other or where emphasis is to be placed. Neither will it give a clear indication of what the teacher aims to do in the subject, what arguments or themes will be developed or what students should know and be able to do at the conclusion of their studies. That is, there should be an indication of what objectives the students will try to fulfill: the amount of factual information to be acquired, skills in reading writing, planning, organizing, or technical skills such as computer literacy, along with any attitudinal changes which will be anticipated outcomes of the course of study. In addition there ought to be an indication of which topics are likely to create difficulties for students and hence form a barrier to their further progress.

I stress the importance of seeking out difficult topics because it is here that more effort may have to be focused in preparing the resource materials—by using a range of media to cover the same topic, for instance—and where the most intensive support in the form of more frequent communication with their teachers may be needed for learners while they are studying the course.

In some cases also, the nature of the course will result in patterns of assessment which present problems for teaching at a distance. For instance, in language learning and mathematical and statistical subjects, frequent testing may be required to ensure understanding of small units of work before proceeding to subsequent units. Using a postal service for submission and return of assignments makes this process difficult, and alternatives such as self-assessment exercises or other means such as electronic mail or facsimile for the submission and return of work may be much more appropriate.

Whereas the humanities and social sciences might once have formed the bulk of courses offered by distance education, an increasing range of courses is now being offered either by distance education alone, or by a combination of distance education and residential attendance. This wider range has implications for the facilities and services necessary for course preparation and ongoing support. For instance, the task of developing teaching materials and support for courses which have heavy practical or clinical components is a particularly challenging one. In some cases, there is a tendency to say that it cannot be done, but in fact there are many examples of successful teaching of courses in science and technology as well as music, art, drama and language. A subject cannot be ruled out for teaching at a distance merely on the grounds that "it can't be done." In some instances this may be true, but in others, given imagination and appropriate resources, the course can be taught effectively.

Course Level

Just as certain subjects were formerly excluded from distance education, teaching at levels beyond a basic first degree was once regarded with some suspicion presumably because of the open-ended nature of objectives at higher levels and because of the greater need for communication and individualized support.

Postgraduate teaching is often seen as different from undergraduate teaching in that it requires:

* opportunities for independent research
* extensive use of library resources

* a high level of report writing
* ongoing discussion with, and guidance from, a supervisor
* frequent opportunities for peer group discussion and group problem solving.

However, objections to higher level teaching at a distance often seem
to be based as much on attitudes towards distance education and on
resource implications, particularly library resources, as on an analysis of
the needs of teaching and learning at this level. At the same time, the
demand for study beyond a first degree is strong, as few people can
afford to take time from work to study full-time on campus beyond their
initial qualifications.

At the other end of the continuum, we should consider to what extent
basic courses at primary and secondary school can be taught effectively
at a distance and how this might be achieved. In some countries, size and
dispersed populations have made education at all levels at a distance a
necessity. Australia and Canada are two examples.

In teaching courses at these levels one confronts again the problem of
how effective communication can be established and maintained between teachers and learners.

Both instances point to a lesser concentration of effort in preparation
of a package of teaching materials for independent study and to a higher
concentration of effort in the support phase with greater individualization than might be the case in courses where a large number of learners
need to acquire basically the same knowledge and meet the same learning objectives.

Student-Related Issues

Consideration of the course to be taught and the institutional context
in which it is embedded needs to be balanced against the likely population of learners. To begin to think about distance education in an impar-
tial way we must put aside some firmly held assumptions about learners
who engage in distance education: (1) that they are always capable of
independent learning and (2) that they desire to be totally free of all
constraints of time and geography. (We also have to reconsider a dominant assumption about teachers in distance education systems: that they
have little need for ongoing communication with students in order to
develop a high level of competence in their profession.)

The basic student-related issues involve consideration of the likely
characteristics of the student population, the level of demand for the

course, the degree to which students will be geographically dispersed, and, in order to establish effective communication links, the extent of their access to technology for communication.

Student Characteristics

Knowledge of the characteristics of the likely population of learners will produce informed decisions about design of resource materials and methods of delivery of the course. Age, gender, ethnic background, socioeconomic background, existing qualifications, present profession, motivation for study, family circumstances, are all variables which are relevant to defining the student population.

If the course is also offered to on-campus students, a first reaction may be that this issue is of little relevance since it is important to maintain parity of instruction. However, maintaining the same standard of instruction in no way implies that the teaching methods used need be identical in both cases. The same content may be covered with the same examination set, but beyond this how the course is taught is an open matter. There seems to be no reason why resource materials should always be identical, why assignments should be the same, or that topics should always be presented in the same sequence, if the student population indicates that a different approach is required.

Heterogeneous populations present problems too, in situations where it is clearly not possible to cater to all individuals needs and approaches to learning. The most appropriate response to this situation is to assume that students will use both the resource materials and support services in diverse ways according to their particular learning needs. There is a good argument, for instance, for developing resource packages with a variety of media and resource materials and also for the provision of a variety of support services. It may well be more economical to use just one medium of instruction and supply a single type of support service, but to do so denies learners the opportunity to match the course of study with their particular learning needs and personal characteristics.

Educational background, and therefore entry level, is also an important issue. In some cases it is likely to range from individuals who are well qualified already to those who have not experienced formal education for several years. If a heterogeneous group of students is anticipated, then multiple entry points may have to be devised or remedial resource materials developed to assist students whose learning skills need to be upgraded or whose basic conceptual level needs to be strengthened.

Projected Demand

An ability to assess the extent of demand for a particular course will enable planners to make informed decisions about how course creation should proceed. Clearly a course which has a low level of demand will not repay the cost of preparation of elaborate resource materials unless these can be used in other ways, for example, to supplement face-to-face instruction. On the other hand, ongoing support will not place an excessive burden on teaching staff under these circumstances. With courses that have a high level of demand the reverse is generally true.

Geographical Distribution

The population of students for a course may be clustered around a central location or may be widely dispersed, and this factor will influence plans for the distribution of resource materials and submission and return of assignment work, but more important, it will determine the kind of communication which is possible on an ongoing bases. If, for example, residential sessions are compulsory then the financial burden of attendance will rest more heavily on more remote students. Even in advanced Western countries, some students may not have ready access to basic communications such as telephhone or post and library services may be nonexistent.

It is in this area of course creation that most imagination is required. There is a tendency to restrict particular services for all students on the basis of the argument that some students will not be able to avail themselves of these services. This opinion is in the interest of equity, but perhaps there are alternative solutions. It may just be the case that different delivery systems need to be devised to cater to students who live in densely populated areas, with the ready access to resources which this implies, than for those whose location is remote.

Low cost communication with learners near a central location must be balanced against high cost communication with more remote students. The access which students who live in cities and large towns have to library resources may be taken for granted whereas special provision may have to be made for remote students, for example by allowing them to access a postal library system. Self-help groups may be formed easily in densely populated regions whereas teleconferencing or individual telephone tuition may be necessary for those who live in small populations.

Access to Technology

The range of technologies that can be used in distance education is very wide indeed, and to some extent teaching methods lag behind what is possible, partly because of the costs of communication and partly because these technologies have not yet permeated the domestic market. If a course requires that students own or have access to a computer of a particular kind then there may be a case for taking the hard decision of not enroling students who cannot meet this requirement. This decision seems to be preferable to deciding to teach the course in ways that cannot fully meet its objectives.

There is another aspect of access though, and that does not concern availability of equipment but does involve familiarity with its use on the part of learners and can present unanticipated barriers to learning and communication with teachers. It would be as well to assume, at least for the current generation of adult learners, that such barriers will exist in a significant number of cases. Hence a component of the course may need to be devoted to simple but effective familiarization processes which ensure that learners have the opportunity to interact with the technology in a nonthreatening way, for instance, at times other than when assessable items are to be submitted using the technology.

SUMMARY.

The transition from mainstream campus-based education to distance education or resource-based education is by no means an automatic process and requires careful planning to be effective. Several facets of institutions which are established primarily to deal with face-to-face instruction of young undergraduates need to be reexamined in the light of proposals to enter into distance education. In particular, infrastructures to support teaching, and costing and funding arrangements, which are usually "taken for granted" aspects of organizations should be be reassessed at an early stage. Likewise detailed attention must be given to the course itself and to the students who will study it at a distance.

The issue of how individual needs will be met, given a large and heterogeneous population of learners, is one which besets most distance education institutions. The variety of resources and opportunities for interaction that are available on campus allows learners to exercise their judgment in effecting a match between their particular learning requirements and resources for learning. There is a good case also for providing a variety of resources and support services for distance education learners as well. Not only are they likely to differ in their approaches to learning but also to have developed established patterns of learning and preferences for certain media and types of communications. The necessity to provide resources must then, in some cases, be balanced against the greater ease of adults in accessing resources in their workplace or communities.

COURSE PREPARATION ISSUES

A consideration of planning issues leads naturally into a discussion of issues that arise in the context of preparing a course for teaching at a distance. These issues are more specific, however, and focus mainly on the selection and creation of appropriate resource materials and on the choice of methods for ongoing communication with learners.

In the first place I will consider the general question of what options are available for preparing a package of resource materials and then consider some criteria on which selection of media for instruction might be based. The issue of scheduling course preparation and delivery will be addressed in the light of the foregoing discussion. Lastly I address the issue of working in teams for course preparation, the strengths and weaknesses of that approach and how some of the pitfalls of a team approach may be avoided.

In the next Section, ongoing support systems will be discussed in greater detail.

Options for Developing Resource Materials

There are several ways of approaching the task of developing a set of distance education materials and it is advisable to consider some viable alternatives at the outset.

In broad terms, materials may either be developed wholly within an institution or use may be made of existing materials from outside sources. No kudos are awarded for developing materials afresh when suitable materials already exist. Such materials may be modified in part to conform to local needs and on the whole this option saves time in course preparation, saves on the cost of production of materials which must be offset against the cost of purchasing the materials, and leaves teachers free to concentrate on other aspects of course delivery. It is still the case though, that most teachers prefer to develop resource materials *de novo*. Here too there are clear advantages in terms of tailoring the materials more closely to teaching and learning needs, avoiding copyright problems and ensuring that the media chosen are the most appropriate for the student population.

Moreover attitudes towards teaching will influence this decision: if this is considered to be a highly personalized experience in which the teacher communicates his or her own original ideas to learners through the resource materials, then using existing materials is unlikely to appeal regardless of the advantages.

A middle road which avoids some of the problems associated with using existing materials and yet saves time on preparation is to collaborate with a colleague or colleagues in preparation of a package of resource materials. These may be colleagues from other institutions who have an interest in mounting the course in their own locations. The possibility of a commercial co-authored publication at some future stage could also be mooted as an outcome of this kind of venture.

THINKING ABOUT MEDIA

In theory, distance educators have a large selection of media alternatives available to them when planning to teach a course. Most media are used somewhere in distance education and information on their use and effectiveness is readily available. However, we should not use a medium just because it is there: the aim is to communicate with that medium, and, in practical terms, the range of media selected in any particular course will depend on several factors:

* the media facilities available in an institution
* emphasis placed on various media by that institution
* cost of the medium
* preference of teachers for working in that medium
* facilities available to the learners to access that medium
* effectiveness of the medium in fulfilling the objectives of the course

Ultimately these are the criteria upon which media selection will be based.

Added to this list we need to look closely at the specific advantages and disadvantages of particular media and the ease with which the subject matter of the course may be translated into those media.

Thus, for instance, while the audiotape is a flexible medium, allowing for varying methods of presentation, and while it is very portable, a good deal of preparation is needed to structure the tape effectively, to script and to secure output of good technical quality. On the part of learners the audio medium may have motivational qualities but if delivered as a lecture they must still take their own notes.

In spite of the suitability of videotapes for demonstrating certain topics to students studying at a distance, making a videotape requires a degree of visual literacy, and specialized assistance is almost always required. The time taken to make a videotape also places a heavy demand on teachers. At the student end, most people are accustomed to using video for entertainment and need to adjust their viewing styles to use the medium for learning purposes.

Computer-based materials are another feasible option for distance education and can provide an active learning experience in students beyond those which are directly related to computing itself. Moreover computers can be used to transmit text or graphics to the learner, to receive assignments and transmit feedback, to provide opportunities for self-assessment. Most problems that occur arise from incompatibility of hardware or software or from a low level of computer literacy among teachers and learners. Moreover, it would be unwise to believe that computer technology can automatically solve educational problems in distance education or any other teaching mode and as with any other medium of instruction a good deal of preparatory activity is needed to use the medium effectively.

Use of printed materials is very common in distance education and both teachers and learners are likely to feel most comfortable with this medium. However a good deal of technical knowledge is required to optimize the effectiveness of this medium, for instance, to create emphasis and to personalize it. On the positive side print is highly portable and accessible as a medium of instruction.

These comments are intended as a stimulus to thinking about the various media in distance education, rather than as an exhaustive discussion of their advantages and disadvantages.

Scheduling Course Preparation and Delivery

Having decided to mount a distance education course and having selected appropriate media for the task, the next step is to draw up a profile for the course and a schedule for course delivery and evaluation. A profile will be useful in a number of ways:

* in seeking approval to offer the course
* to enable teachers and others associated with course delivery to see clearly what tasks lie ahead
* to budget for materials preparation and ongoing support.

Basically a profile will consist of five sections:

1. Course details
2. Details of learning materials package
3. Details of ongoing support activities for learners, including assessment
4. Human and technical resource implications
5. Budget estimate for the course

A schedule for course preparation and delivery can then be developed to accompany the profile and estimates must be made as to the time that various activities will occupy.

The time required to produce a package of resource materials obviously depends on a large number of variables including the nature of the subject matter, the media employed, availability of support staff, production facilities and the work habits and commitments of teachers. Hence there is little point in attempting to suggest norms for course preparation, but in general terms teachers who are relieved of all other teaching and administrative duties should be able to fulfill their part of the task of course preparation in about six months, whereas at least twelve months should be allocated if other duties must be carried as well.

In addition, deadlines have to be built in for text processing, instructional design input, production of audiovisual materials, computer software, library orders and any other special requirements associated with the course.

Teaching procedures will depend very much on the course, students and the arrangements which an institution makes for support services. It is advisable to schedule teaching activities at the same time as a package of materials is being prepared so that when they receive the materials, learners have a clear idea of what will be expected of them. In particular consideration should be given to:

* the assessment pattern, particularly as it is affected by turnaround times due to mailing, handling and marking of assignments
* regional activities such as tutorials and study schools
* campus-based sessions
* telephone tutorials
* visits to regional centers by teaching staff

Lastly it is advisable to decide whether an evaluation of the course will be conducted in order to obtain feedback about its effectiveness. Before deciding to do an evaluation, it is a good idea to consider why it might be necessary. For instance, matters to review are: if the course is offered by distance education for the first time, if it is due for revision, if new media components have been introduced, if there have been a large number of queries or complaints, if the course has had an unusually high withdrawal or failure rate.

If the results of the evaluation are to be worthwhile, consideration should be given to how the collected data will be analyzed and used. If circumstances will prevent teachers from taking appropriate action then it may be better to delay the evaluation until a more suitable time.

Working In Teams

One possible course development model uses teams to plan course creation and prepare learning materials. This model implies role diversification where the team consists of teachers and a number of nonteaching professionals as well. There are advantages in working this way in that the workload is divided among several staff members and the course can be enhanced both by the sharing of expertise and by jointly developing ideas for teaching it. Pitfalls as well must be considered before deciding to adopt a team approach.

Where teams are institutionalized such as at the British Open University, they are claimed to provide opportunities for staff development, to enhance the quality of materials produced and in general to foster a collegial atmosphere. On the other hand, not all teams function well; it is time consuming and sometimes exhausting and not all teachers feel comfortable with the team approach.

Conditions exist where a team approach will clearly not work, for instance, if commitment to this approach is lacking amongst the members of the team. This commitment means a willingness to attend meetings regularly, to abide by decisions made by the group, to collaborate with others, to meet deadlines and to accept the comments made on one's work by other team members. Teams create the additional problem of who actually owns the final outcome and who has responsibility for the course and its students.

Whereas working in teams in face-to-face teaching is fairly straightforward because teachers agree on the structure of the course, allocate responsibility for lectures and assignment marking and proceed in a fairly independent manner from then on, working in a team to prepare a distance education course requires close liaison and consultation among team members. The following suggestions may prove helpful in ensuring a successful outcome.

1. At the outset elect a chairperson who will agree to assume responsibility for:
   * calling regular meetings of the team and monitoring progress
   * monitoring the student workload imposed by the team as a whole
   * preparing a course overview for student use
   * submission of materials on time to the production unit
   * negotiating with other units such as the printing office
   * ensuring that all books have been ordered
2. Team members should agree what responsibilities they will take on in preparing resource materials and in subsequent revisions.
3. An evaluation questionnaire may need to be designed which allows parts of the course to be evaluated separately from the overall impact of the course.

The team is one way to come to terms with the task of course creation and of staff development but it is not the only way. For instance, increasing opportunities for contact between teachers and learners, employment of appropriate support staff to assist individual teachers, recognition by an institution of the time necessary for course preparation and revision of existing courses, recognition of the efforts of teachers in producing teaching materials will all contribute to a positive attitude towards distance education and to the development of courses of good quality.

ONGOING SUPPORT FOR LEARNERS IN DISTANCE EDUCATION

The most significant advance in distance education in the past decade is the degree to which technology has made it possible for teachers and learners to communicate directly and for learners to communicate among themselves. Such developments include audio, video and computer conferencing, electronic mail, facsimile transmission. Such communication can take place via telephone lines or by satellite. The effect is either to speed up the transmission of one-way communication say via facsimile or electronic mail or to establish two-way or multipoint communication which enables interaction to take place in real time.

Many areas of teaching could be affected, such as faster submission and return of assignments through electronic mail of facsimile, scheduling of regular tutorials for small group work, handling administrative and academic queries from students, informing students of changes to the course as it proceeds, allowing access to library resources and indexes, allowing access to course information from a range of institutions through a database, personal counselling.

Yet in many countries costs remain a barrier to implementation of systems which take full advantage of the opportunities that exist. It seems that for most education systems either government support is needed or a "user pays" system must be adopted.

When contemplating these initiatives in distance education it is important to consider both costs and benefits, however. Costs might include:

1. Cost of reconfiguring an existing infrastructure for distance education which is currently directed towards production of self-instructional resource materials.
2. Cost of purchasing, installing and maintaining new equipment such as a teleconference bridge or satellite receiver.
3. Cost of transmission time.
4. Cost of allocating space in existing buildings to accommodate the new forms of communication.

On the side of benefits, however, we might consider:

1. The range of participants who might begin to engage in distance education, particularly those for whom learning primarily from self-instructional materials is inappropriate: young children, postgraduate students, people who are not oriented towards print, learners who need support and direction in their study.
2. The positive effect on teachers who might well begin to utilize the interactive skills they have acquired in face-to-face teaching in distance education and do not wish to make the transition to media based teaching which places heavy emphasis on the preparation of instructional materials.
3. The flexibility which such systems might permit teachers in terms of developing a course of study while in the act of teaching, say by agreeing with learners to change direction, change assessment requirements and so on, according to the specific needs that learners express.
4. Establishment of a more personal relationship between teachers and learners.
5. Enabling courses to be offered to small groups without a heavy initial investment in preparation of resource materials.

CONCLUSION

Clearly it is beyond the scope of this chapter to explore all the issues that surround course creation within distance education and resource-based teaching or indeed to examine individual issues in great depth. What I have attempted to do is to highlight those considerations which, if not taken into account at the outset, may well frustrate attempts to mount an effective distance education program.

It is clear from this discussion that, while technical knowledge is necessary to the distance education enterprise, and while the contribution of nonteaching professionals should be clearly recognized, the essence of a successful operation resides in the institutional context in which the program will be embedded.

Very often the onus of creating an effective distance education course rests on individual teachers and support staff such as instructional designers and editors. Clearly these individuals do bear a responsibility for the final outcome. The talents and enthusiasm of teachers and other professionals can well be frustrated, however, if their efforts do not receive official recognition, if appropriate funding is not available and if an infrastructure does not exist where distance education can be carried out.

At a time when the possibilities for developing effective distance education systems are expanding rapidly, a basic choice must be made concerning the kind of infrastructure that best serves distance education in particular institutions. Some existing models might point towards a heavy investment in preparation of self-instructional materials for course delivery but present indications are that there are advantages to be gained in considering the alternative investment in means of direct communication.

REFERENCES

Communications Technology

Abe, Y. (1988). Communications technology. In D. Sewart and J. S. Daniel (Eds.), *Developing Distance Education* (pp. 9–15). International Council for Distance Education, Oslo.

Bates, A. W. (1984). Selecting and designing low-cost media for distance education. *Papers on Information Technology,* No. 238. Open University: Milton Keynes.

Collins, V. A. C. & Murphy, P. J. (1988). A new adult student: Learning by interactive satellite. In D. Sewart and J. S. Daniel (Eds.), *Developing Dis-*

tance Education (pp. 112–115). International Council for Distance Education, Oslo.

Foks, J. (1988). Distance education—a developing concept. In D. Sewart and J. S. Daniel (Eds.), *Developing Distance Education* (pp. 31–38). International Council for Distance Education, Oslo.

Garrison, D. R. (1985). Three generations of technological innovations in distance education. *Distance Education, 6*(2), 235–241.

Hall, J. (1987). Bridging the technology-pedagogy gap. In P. Smith and M. Kelly (Eds.), *Distance Education and the Mainstream: Convergence in Education* (pp. 44–56). Croom Helm: London.

Robertson, B. (1987). Audio teleconferencing: Low cost technology for external studies networking. *Distance Education, 8*(1), 121–130.

Rothe, J. P. (1985). Audio teleconferencing and distance education: Towards a conceptual synthesis. *Distance Education, 6*(2), 199–208.

Shobe, C. R. (1986). New technologies in distance education. In I. Mugridge and D. Kaufman (Eds.), *Distance Education in Canada* (pp. 283–295). Croom Helm: London.

Smith, P. (1987). Distance education and educational change. In P. Smith and M. Kelly (Eds.), *Distance Education and the Mainstream: Convergence in Education* (pp. 24–43). Croom Helm: London.

Guiton, P. (1982). Resource allocation in the Australian two-mode university. In J. S. Daniel, M. A. Stroud & J. R. Thompson (Eds.), *Learning at a Distance: A World Perspective* (pp. 176–178). Athabasca University/International Council for Correspondence Education, Edmonton.

Rumble, G. (1986). Activity costing in mixed-mode institutions: A report based on a study of Deakin University. *Deakin Open Education Monograph,* No. 2. Geelong, Victoria.

Rumble, G. (1988). Economics in distance education: Time for a change of direction? In D. Sewart and J. S. Daniel (Eds.), *Developing Distance Education* (pp. 63–69). International Council for Distance Education, Oslo.

Course Content

Dohner, C. W. et al. (1985). Teaching basic science and clinical medicine at a distance: An evaluation of satellite communication. *Distance Education, 6*(1), 4–33.

Guillamon, J. R. & Guillamon, A. (1985). Teaching psycho-biology at a distance. *Distance Education, 6*(1), 68–78.

Shott, M. (1985). Teaching physics at a distance. *Distance Education, 5*(1), 102–127.

Course Teams

Crick, M. (1980). Course teams: Myth and actuality. *Distance Education, 1*(2), 127–141.

Kelly, M. E. (1987). Course teams and instructional design in Australian distance education: A reply to Shaw and Taylor. *Distance Education, 8*(1), 106–120.

Shaw, B. & Taylor, J. (1984). Instructional design: Distance education and academic tradition. *Distance Education, 5*(2), 277–285.

Stringer, M. (1980). Lifting the course team curse. *Teaching at a Distance, 18*, 13–16.

Tight, M. (1985). Do we really need course teams? *Teaching at a Distance, 23*, 48–50.

Models of Distance Education

Ljosa, E. & Willen, B. (1984). Small-scale and large-scale organisational models of distance education: A discussion. *Distance Education, 5*(1), 108–111.

Neil, M. W. (Ed.) (1983). *Education of adults at a distance.* Kogan Page: London.

Smith, K. (1980). Course development procedures. *Distance Education, 1*(1), 61–67.

Student Characteristics

Hough, M. (1984). Motivation of adults: Implications of adult learning theories for distance education. *Distance Education, 5*(1), 7–23.

Marland, P. et al. (1984). Learning from distance teaching materials: A study of students mediating responses. *Distance Education, 5*(2), 215–236.

McDonald, R. & Knights, S. (1979). Learning from tapes: The experience of home-based students. *Programmed Learning and Educational Technology, 16*(1), 46–51.

Morgan, A., Taylor, E. & Gibbs, G. (1982). Understanding the distance learner as a whole person. In J. S. Daniel, M. A. Stroud, & J. R. Thompson (Eds.), *Learning at a Distance: A World Perspective* (pp. 103–106). Athabasca University/International Council for Correspondence Education, Edmonton.

Thompson, G. (1984). The cognitive style of field-dependence as an explanatory construct in distance education dropout. *Distance Education, 5*(2), 286–293.

Student Support Services

McInnis-Rankin, E. & Brindley, J. (1986). Student support services. In I. Mugridge and D. Kaufman (Eds.), *Distance Education in Canada* (pp. 60–80). Croom Helm: London.

Paul, R. (1988). If student services are so important, then why are we cutting them back? In D. Sewart and J. S. Daniel (Eds.), *Developing Distance Education* (pp. 50–56). International Council for Distance Education, Oslo.

Sewart, D. (1981). Distance teaching: A contradiction in terms? *Teaching at a Distance, 19*, 8–18.

Post-Graduate Teaching

Bynner, J. (1986). Masters teaching in education by distance methods. *Distance Education, 7*(1) 23–37.

Jarvis, B. (1982). Taught higher degrees. *Teaching at a Distance, 21*(2), 76–78.

White, M. A. (1980). Graduate degrees by external study: Nova University programmes in Florida. *Distance Education, 1*(2), 188–197.

CHAPTER 8

AUDIO TELECONFERENCING DESIGN AND DELIVERY

D. Randy Garrison

Audio teleconferencing was described in Chapter 4 as a "new genera-tion" of distance education in spite of its having existed for quite a while. Audio teleconferencing makes possible not only immediate two-way conversation but it also is a group method of distance education. Stu-dents are no longer required to study in relative isolation. With audio teleconferencing students are extended the opportunity to freely commu-nicate at a distance in a "classroom" context. The significance of these characteristics is just beginning to be fully recognized and that is why audio teleconferencing can be regarded as a new generation technology.

Audio teleconferencing is not an industrialized form of distance educa-tion and therefore does not offer the cost benefits of mass distribution. However, the other side of this coin is that for small and widely dispersed target audiences it provides a greater cost advantage compared to the high costs of designing and producing a self-instructional resource package. But it is not cost analyses in the end which will justify audio teleconferenc-ing or distance education in general. It is what it offers in supporting and facilitating the educational transaction. The distinct advantage of audio teleconferencing upon which design and delivery considerations are based is that it is analogous to the traditional classroom and therefore has a capacity for interaction (see Chapter 3). This in turn makes it more likely to be adopted by traditional campus-based institutions.

The purpose of this chapter is to outline system design and course delivery issues involving audio teleconferencing. System design will ad-dress macro-level infrastructure and planning issues. Course delivery and instructional design concerns will be the focus of the latter part of the chapter. Parenthetically, it should be noted that teleconferencing can be very effective in conducting meetings. The use is common in the business sector and demands a knowledge of special techniques. How-ever, while business use is a very important application of teleconferencing, we will confine our discussions to audio teleconferencing in the educational setting.

SYSTEM DESIGN

Technically, there are a variety of ways to initiate an audio tele-conference. Olgren and Parker (1983) describe the four major types as user-initiated, dial-up, "meet-me" teleconference, and a dedicated net-work. The user-initiated teleconference simply makes use of a standard telephone with a three-way call feature. Like the first type, the dial-up conference uses a public telephone network but is set-up by the tele-phone operator. While the cost may be somewhat higher, a larger num-ber of people can be connected and voice quality controlled better than the user-initiated. In "meet-me" teleconferencing, participants call into the bridge from a location convenient to them and, therefore, an audio teleconference can be set-up in a shorter period of time than a dial-up conference. This system uses a public network, and many people at several sites may participate. Audio bridging services are available through private companies as well as educational organizations. A dedi-cated private network uses leased transmission lines connecting a num-ber of fixed locations. For extensive use of teleconferencing this may prove to be cost-effective.

The first three types of audio teleconferencing make it possible for a new user to try the system out in a reasonably inexpensive manner. As such, technology is not usually a major concern when planning a pilot study of audio teleconferencing. While considerable organization is re-quired up-front, audio teleconferencing, even on a regular basis, is very cost effective due to readily available technological hardware and mini-mal additional infrastructure.

In addition to bridging equipment and transmission lines other infra-structure requirements are teleconferencing rooms, speaker and micro-phones, and possible audiographic enhancements. A teleconference room can be a regular classroom, board room, or office that has a telephone line into it. From the telephone outlet a speaker and micro-phones are attached. Depending on the need, a variety of audiographic enhancements may be added. Three of the more common types are described in Chapter 4.

To reduce the number of technological glitches and ensure a quality teleconference several support personnel are normally required. The two most important are the bridge operator and the local teleconference assistant (LTA). The bridge operator will ensure that all locations are connected and that the voice quality is optimized. The teacher then is not concerned with these matters and should only have to deal with the instructional transaction. Similarly the LTA is needed to set-up the equipment and handle any technological problems that may arise. Students must be allowed to concentrate only upon the educational process and not be distracted by the technology. The LTA may perform a variety of additional functions such as distributing materials, collecting assignments, and invigilating exams.

Now that we have some idea of the technology that is required to support an audio teleconference we turn to the reasons for selecting this method of distance education. It has already been stated that from a cost perspective audio teleconferencing can be attractive to educational organizations with limited financial resources for distance education. Another issue is the acceptability of the delivery technology by the teachers and larger organizations. Again we noted previously that, generally speaking, audio teleconferencing may have a better chance of being accepted than other distance education technologies that may demand greater individual initiative of the student.

However, once we break through the technological and acceptance threshold, it is the educational issues that must be addressed. That is, how effective is this method of delivering education at a distance considering various curriculum and student factors. As Kelly has mentioned in the previous chapter, each educational situation represents a unique context of curriculum and learner needs which suggests the development of unique systems—not just the blind application of whatever technology is available.

From an educational perspective, audio teleconferencing is a unique example of delivering education at a distance because of the opportunity for dialogue, negotiation, and validation of knowledge. What it gives up, however, is a degree of autonomy on the part of the learner. The loss of convenience in terms of time and travel are more than compensated for by the opportunity for interaction, the flexibility regarding availability of techniques, and the pacing capabilities of audio teleconferencing. Notwithstanding these strong educational attributes, Wagner and Reddy (1987) state that "just because teleconferencing is able to deliver interactive educational programming over great distances does not necessarily mean that teleconferencing is generically suitable for the delivery of all instruction" (p. 49). They go on to suggest that it is important to understand the types of learning outcomes if teleconferencing is to be used to its full instructional potential.

As Winn has stated in Chapter 5, media may not affect how well individuals learn but they can influence the efficiency of delivering instruction. This is true of audio teleconferencing. Audio teleconferencing generally may be more efficient than correspondence from a learning perspective, but it may not be ideally suited to delivering specific content without the enhancement of other media. And in some situations it may never replace the need for face-to-face contact. What then can we say about selecting audio teleconferencing for delivering education at a distance?

The strength of audio teleconferencing is clearly its attribute of enabling discussion among participants who are verbally proficient. For this reason it is particularly suited to higher level cognitive tasks such as problem solving and values clarification. Upper undergraduate and postgraduate university level courses are often very adaptable to audio teleconferencing. It makes possible greater individualization and personalization of the educational experience through true negotiation of goals and immediate recognition of knowledge acquisition. In general, courses which are enhanced by group discussion and students who are able to express themselves well are ideally suited for audio teleconferencing.

Audio teleconferencing's strength of keeping participants on task may also be a serious weakness in some situations. That is, it may not be the most satisfactory choice for "tasks which are of a complex nature, or which involve interpersonal factors" (Fowler & Wackerbarth, 1980, p. 247). However, other than face-to-face instruction, audio teleconferencing may be the first and only viable choice if distance delivery is required. If audio teleconferencing is used to deliver large amounts of information it will in fact be turned into a one-way communication medium. While it is quite capable of delivering information, students find it tedious and boring. Therefore, courses which consist largely of transmitting information and do not demand extensive explanation or discussion may best be delivered by another technology.

We are not at the point where we can rely on definitive design criteria in selecting and using audio teleconferencing. This is due to the inherent communication (educational) strengths of audio teleconferencing, the flexibility of this technology to be enhanced by other media, and the opportunity to incorporate and build upon the many strengths of correspondence study. That is, audio teleconferencing is very adaptable and can combine the basic advantages of correspondence information transfer as well as enhance its communication capabilities with other media and technology. Beyond design issues, however, the key to successful audio teleconferencing is to use the method to its full potential from a communication and instructional perspective.

INSTRUCTIONAL CONSIDERATIONS

In correspondence education considerable effort is given to the design phase. With audio teleconference the emphasis is upon the delivery or instructional phase. It is the educational transaction or what the student does with the course content that takes precedent. For this reason it is essential that the principles of facilitating an audio teleconference are understood. These principles will be discussed under the issues of climate setting, presentation, participation, and evaluation.

In adult education considerable emphasis is placed upon creating a climate conducive to learning. This is even more of a concern in audio teleconferencing due to the technological interface and students not being able to see the teacher or a majority of the other students. If interaction is to be achieved it will start by reducing anxiety and providing support. Some of the ways to create a secure climate are: attend to the physical arrangements, provide introductory materials, help students get to know each other, have the teacher allow his/her personality to show, and use a roll call to start each class.

While physical requirements are at a minimum, it is necessary to have an attractive room with a large table to arrange microphones and speaker as well as enough room for the students to sit comfortably with their learning materials. Some minimal instruction should be given regarding the operation of the microphones. Introductory materials might include a welcome letter, biography and picture of the instructor, list of centers and other students, outline of the first session, as well as the visual course related information. While introductions are important the focus of the first session should be on the course and the instructor. More extensive "get acquainted" activities may best be left to the second session. The key individual, of course, is the teacher who must explain his/her style and expectations and model the open and interactive techniques so essential to a successful audio teleconference and good educational practice in general.

The overriding issue related to presentation is to be organized and to communicate this organization to the class. Generally speaking content should be delivered to the student before the teleconference class. The teacher may provide an overview but should involve the group as soon as possible. Not spending too much time on any one activity will maintain attention. Repeating and summarizing content both verbally and with print will help to ensure the message has been received. Other media such as an overhead, video tapes and audiographic devices will also maintain interest and attention. When ending a teleconference session it is important not only to summarize what was accomplished but also to describe preparatory activities and assignments for the next session.

Audio teleconferencing is an interactive medium and if it is not used primarily as such, it will not be effective. To a large extent audio teleconferencing encourages the good educational techniques described in Chapter 3. Without the active participation of the students, teleconferencing is not likely to be a satisfying and worthwhile experience for them. Virtually any technique used in a traditional classroom setting may be used in audio teleconferencing. This capability is what makes it such a powerful method of delivering education at a distance. Participation need not be limited to the teacher and student. Group discussions may occur with local groups interacting amongst themselves or via electronically linking two or more sites with a bridge. Another interesting possibility is the opportunity to interview well known individuals or dialogue with other resource people for the cost of a telephone call. In a pragmatic sense, participation is necessary to know what students are thinking and doing because visual communication is unlikely.

The fourth area to consider in teleconferencing is evaluation. Both formative and summative content evaluation can be done conveniently. The only additional concern for formal evaluation in an audio teleconferencing course would be to have exams delivered and supervised at the local site. Informal evaluation would be incorporated in the ongoing participation activities or specifically with question and answer sessions.

CONCLUSION

The guidelines and suggestions for designing and delivering an audio teleconference incorporate the educational principles of dialogue, negotiation, and validation of knowledge. Audio teleconferencing makes it very easy to adopt and implement appropriate educational techniques. In fact, if collaborative and interactive techniques are not used then audio teleconferencing is not likely to be a successful method of delivering education at a distance. When audio teleconferencing is combined and enhanced with media such as a telewriter system (which can provide interactive visual information comparable to the blackboard and overhead projector) there are few courses that could not be delivered in an academically sound manner.

This chapter provides only a brief introduction and outline of considerations in designing and delivering an audio teleconference. Much effort must be put into orienting and training the teachers as to the necessity of active participation and how to encourage interaction. From a broader planning perspective considerable thought should also to be given to the integration of a variety of technology and media to best meet the demands of the curriculum as well as the students' needs. This is the focus of the next chapter.

REFERENCES

Fowler, G. D., & Wackerbarth, M. E. (1980). Audio teleconferencing versus face-to-face conferencing: A synthesis of the literature. *The Western Journal of Speech Communication, 44,* 236–252.

Olgren, C. H., & Parker, L. A. (1983). *Teleconferencing technology and applications.* Dedham, MA: Artech House.

Wagner, E. D., & Reddy, N. L. (1987). Design considerations in selecting teleconferencing for instruction. *The American Journal of Distance Education, 1*(3), 49–56.

CHAPTER 9

THE INTEGRATION OF VIDEO-BASED INSTRUCTION

Charlotte Gunawardena

Recent developments in video-based technologies have made a significant impact on distance education systems by offering viable, alternative means for delivering instruction at a distance. In the United States, postsecondary educational institutions offering courses at a distance have had to deal with issues related to the selection and integration of these new delivery systems not only in an effort to reach the distant learner, but also in an effort to maintain a competitive edge over other providers of adult continuing and professional education.

This chapter delineates video-based delivery technologies that have relevance for distance education. It also provides guidelines for the integration of video-based instruction into preproduced distance education courses.

VIDEO-BASED TECHNOLOGIES

Video-based technologies have unique characteristics and capabilities. Each technology differs in the way it delivers instruction and influences learning. Willen (1988) discusses three important characteristics of a delivery medium that have an impact on learning: the ability of the medium to reach all students, the flexibility it affords the learner, and the extent to which it provides two-way communication. Delivery and student access relate to how the technology distributes the learning material to distant learners and their locations: homes, places of work, or local study centers. Flexibility refers to the extent to which the medium permits learners to use it at a time, place and manner convenient for them. In other words, how much control the learner has over the medium. Two-way communication capability focuses on the degree to which the technology permits interaction between the teacher and the student.

Although video-based technologies can deliver the instructional message or material in a variety of ways, they can be broadly classified into four main categories in terms of their application to distance education: (a) preproduced television programs, (b) televised instruction, (c) interactive video, and (d) videoconferencing.

(a) *Preproduced television programs* comprise the video component of a videocourse or telecourse usually delivered via open-broadcast, cable or satellite transmission. These programs are also distributed in recorded form on videocassettes. A telecourse usually consists of about 25 to 30 half-hour preproduced television programs, a textbook and a study guide.

An advantage to using preproduced television programs of broadcast quality is that they can exploit the unique "symbolic" or "presentational" characteristics of the medium that distinguish television from other kinds of media. Bates (1987) observes that television is a rich medium in terms of the density of information, because of the amount of symbol systems (iconic, digital and analog coding systems) it can simultaneously carry. "It is the only medium which combines words, still and moving pictures, events occurring in real time, slow or accelerated motion, animation, and even text. This gives it a power to present information that other media lack" (p. 6). By exploiting these features unique to the medium, television programs can teach in a different way from a classroom lecture.

However, while professional broadcast production can take advantage of the unique "presentational" characteristics of television, it distances the instructor from the production and often presents problems related to the integration of television programs with the rest of the course material.

Preproduced telecourses are most often assembled by professional producers and distributed via open-broadcast television using a Public Broadcasting Station (PBS). The great advantage is that these courses can be delivered directly to the homes of a large number of students. Despite its ability to reach a large section of the student population, open-broadcast television is a one-way communication medium which does not provide for interaction (two-way communication) between the student and teacher. Since students cannot question the instructor to clarify problems, and since professional broadcast production "makes the learner dependent on 'responsible' broadcasting" (Bates 1983, p. 61), this system of distribution can encourage passive acceptance of the instruction. To make the system interactive, open-broadcast distribution requires an added system to provide an audio (telephone) return circuit. Cable television (one-way, without telephone feedback), another system frequently employed to deliver preproduced television programs, suffers from most of the instructional weaknesses associated with broadcast television.

Communications satellites have revolutionized television delivery by having the capacity to transmit television signals to earth stations of distributing broadcast television, and the limitations associated with open-broadcast deliveries remain.

Students hardly have control over the medium with open-broadcast and cable (one-way) deliveries. Bates (1984) has observed that "broadcasts are ephemeral, cannot be reviewed, are uninterruptable, and are presented at the same pace for all students. A student cannot reflect upon an idea or pursue a line of thought during a program, without losing the thread of the program itself. A student cannot go over the same material several times until it is understood" (p. 31). Therefore, it is difficult for the learner to integrate or relate broadcast material to other learning. Hence, the need for broadcast programming to be accompanied by support materials in the form of prebroadcast notes and follow-up exercises and activities.

Access to videocassette recorders, however, has enabled students to overcome not only the limitations of inconvenient broadcast schedules but also the lack of control over television programs. Students can exercise "control" over the programming by using the stop, rewind, replay, and fast forward features to proceed at their own pace. Video-cassettes are very versatile as they provide flexibility and student control over them.

If videocassettes are designed to take advantage of their control characteristics, then there is opportunity for students to interact with the lesson material by repeating until they master it and by reflecting on and analyzing the information. The control features that videocassettes afford the learner give course designers the ability to integrate video segments more closely with other learning materials so that learners can move between lesson material supplied by different media. Recorded television programs, therefore, offer the learner and the instructor more control in the way video material can be used for learning purposes.

(b) *Televised instruction* is a relay or transmission of a televised classroom lecture to an off-campus location, usually with an audio-feedback system (telephone) that permits live interaction between the student and instructor. In this delivery system, only the technology of television transmission is used, not the "presentational" characteristics unique to the medium. The great advantage of this type of delivery is that it provides for live interaction between the student, the instructor and other students, and offers the student a certain degree of control over the medium by allowing him or her to ask questions from the instructor and receive feedback. However, if there are several off-campus sites receiving the same lecture, the amount of time available for a student to interact with the instructor is limited.

Instructional Television Fixed Service (ITFS), sometimes referred to as closed circuit television and point-to-point microwave are two systems that extend the campus classroom. These systems are usually one-way video and two-way audio. The televised lecture originates from a "studio classroom" on campus and students at remote locations have to be present at a receiving site to participate in the lecture. They can question the instructor during the class through a talkback telephone system or with a FM microwave technology called radio talkback, and the question is heard both by on-campus and off-campus class members. Fiber optics delivery systems that can simultaneously provide voice, video and data transmissions and two-way communication are beginning to revolutionze the way on-campus classrooms are delivered to remote locations.

(c) *Interactive Video* is the combination of computer and video technologies, where it is possible by computer control of a videodisc or videocassette player to obtain random access to recorded video sequences which allow the individual user a significant degree of interaction with the lesson material. The interaction between the learner and the lesson material is provided by the computer program. Interactive video systems that have a built-in electronic mail component allow the learner at a remote site to communicate with an on-campus instructor.

Interactive video has great potential for education and training with its ability to deliver individualized, interactive instruction affording the learner significant control over the medium. However, its use by post-secondary distance education institutions is likely to be limited because of the very high cost of production. It has potential for development where students can get to a learning center to use the system, or where industry can provide access to a system at the workplace.

(d) *Videoconferencing* is more of a concept than a technology. It is a meeting that takes place between individuals or groups located at different distant sites. Full motion videoconferencing permits live interaction between distant locations via one-way or two-way video and two-way audio. The system provides visual images similar to broadcast television, using a single technology like point-to-point microwave or combinations of two or more technologies, such as ITFS and regular telephone service.

Satellite technology has given a new impetus to videoconferencing by having the capability to transmit television signals from the originating site to numerous locations scattered over large geographical areas. The most common form of videoconferencing in distance education is one-way satellite television transmission with terrestrial telephone allowing students to call in (voice only) to the broadcast. Videoconferencing can make a great contribution especially in the delivery of current and updated information to specialized groups such as doctors, nurses, engineers and teachers scattered over large geographical areas. Videoconferences can be videotaped for those who are unable to participate in the live conference.

A survey (Gunawardena, 1988) of postsecondary educational institutions in the United States that deliver instruction via video-based technologies indicated the predominant use of three kinds of systems: noninteractive open-broadcast and cable systems, and videocassette recordings. These three systems will be the dominant video-based delivery technologies in the near future. When the delivery technologies are noninteractive, as in the first two, other provision must be made for interaction among the distant learner, the instructor, and the instructional materials.

VIDEO-BASED INSTRUCTION AND SUPPORT

When designing and developing video-based courses, especially for distance learners, it is all too easy to focus attention on the content of what is to be taught and pay little attention to how learning can be facilitated. Instructional designers and developers need to consider the teaching-learning process of a distance education system and be mindful of the relationship that exists between the instructor, the student and the content.

Waniewicz (1972) has pointed out that media cannot by themselves provide for learner needs such as supervision, guidance, additional clarification, and verification of results. In order to consolidate and extend their impact they must be accompanied by support and follow-up devices of one form or another.

Support services provide the two-way communication necessary in a distance learning system. Holmberg (1981), has pointed out that "noncontiguous interaction" (p. 12) between the student and the instructor can take place in two ways: (a) real communication in writing, on the telephone, or face-to-face, and (b) simulated communication ("mediated form of guided didactic conversation" (p. 12)) in the form of self-assessment and self-remediation exercises, or assignments for submission which are commented on and returned to the students with constructive advice.

Support can take many forms. Gunawardena's survey (1988) indicated that forms of student support considered very helpful by institutions using video-based instruction, fall into four categories: (a) guidelines for studying—the study guide, (b) interaction—telephone office hours for faculty, and telephone calls initiated by faculty, (c) Feedback—individualized feedback from faculty and computerized feedback, and (d) access to library resources. These four kinds of support present means to integrate a video component into a distance teaching system.

Hodgson (1986) notes that support systems contribute to the "process" of a course as do the learning materials, but that they are rarely studied as an integrated part of the process. Generally, research has focussed either on the design and development of learning materials or the role and function of support systems. She stresses the need to look at the interrelationship between a distance learning course's support systems and its learning materials, and the influence this relationship has upon students' experiences and approaches to learning.

There is considerable debate, however, regarding to what extent the distance learner needs to be supported. It can be argued that adult students choose a preproduced distance study course (which may contain a combination of videotapes, audiocassettes, textbooks and study guides), because it is intended to be self-instructional, that is, it is accessible for independent study without the support of an instructor. Therefore, they may not need the support of an instructor to guide, direct and assist them in achieving their goals.

However, it is difficult to assume that all adult students who enroll in distance education courses are self-directed learners, who have acquired "learning-how-to-learn" capabilities and have the ability to maintain active control of the learning process. Most students need guidance and support. Therefore, it is necessary to provide support services for the distant learner to facilitate the teaching-learning process and these support services must be combined with the learning materials and the instructional delivery media. Support is crucial if a major portion of the instruction is delivered via a noninteractive medium such as open-broadcast television. The student, however, should be able to decide on how much use to make of the support offered.

Salomon and Leigh (cited in Wohl and Tidhar, 1988) have argued that the viewer who has found television an "everyday affair" and "easy" to receive invests little time in active processing. They have noted that "preconceptions of the medium of one's self-efficacy in handling it satisfactorily are related to effort invested in processing its material and to inferential learning" (p. 12). When dealing with television, the Amount of Invested Mental Effort (AIME) is low. Therefore, unless students are "specifically instructed to treat a television stimulus differently than usual, they invest little effort in it and extract little inferential knowledge from it" (p. 12).

Therefore, when a television program is chosen as one medium of instruction in a preproduced distance education course, instructional strategies and support services should be provided to help students learn from the video material and integrate it with information conveyed by the rest of the course components.

STRATEGIES FOR INTEGRATING VIDEO-BASED INSTRUCTION INTO DISTANCE EDUCATION COURSES

Bates (1983) has observed that television has two functions in the learning process: (a) to maximize the knowledge acquired by presenting information in a different way from the presentation of the same information through another medium, and (b) to develop certain mental skills (information-processing skills) in using knowledge.

A model (Figure 1) has been proposed to formulate guidelines for helping adult students learn from the television programs in a pre-produced distance-study course, and for integrating the video instruction with other materials in that course (Gunawardena, 1988). Strategies for facilitating learning discussed in the model focus both on the acquisition of knowledge and the development of mental skills.

A review of literature related to (a) adult learning and current learning theories, (b) learning from television, and (c) the nature of distance learning, provided the theoretical base for the instructional strategies and support services described in the model. The survey of 49 post-secondary educational institutions in the United States supplied information on the effectiveness of instructional strategies and support services used to integrate video-based instruction.

The model is influenced by the information processing view of learning and Gagne's (1977) conception of instruction; the arrangement of events external to the learner in order "to activate, to support, and to maintain the internal processing that constitutes each learning event" (p. 24). The model draws on two views of instruction: Gagne's (1977) model of the "relations between phases of learning and events of instruction," and Wohl and Tidhar's (1988) "macro and micro integrative teaching system of television viewing."

The model consists of three stages which follow a natural sequence: before viewing the television program, during the television program, and after viewing the television program. The final stage provides for the "integration" of the television viewing experience. It is here that the

Figure 1

A Model for the Integration of Video-Based Instruction

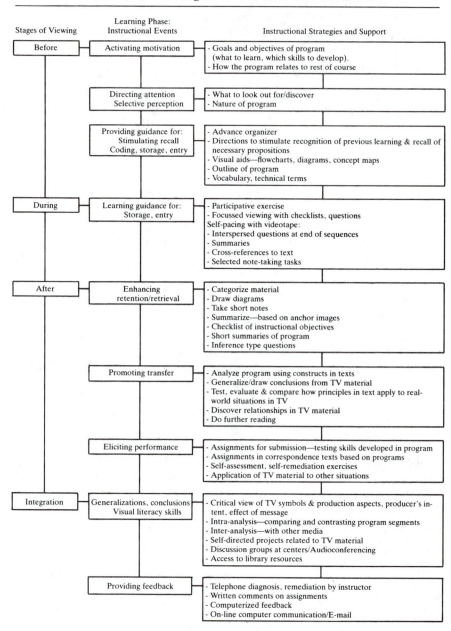

Stages of Viewing	Learning Phase: Instructional Events	Instructional Strategies and Support
Before	Activating motivation	- Goals and objectives of program (what to learn, which skills to develop). - How the program relates to rest of course
	Directing attention Selective perception	- What to look out for/discover - Nature of program
	Providing guidance for: Stimulating recall Coding, storage, entry	- Advance organizer - Directions to stimulate recognition of previous learning & recall of necessary propositions - Visual aids—flowcharts, diagrams, concept maps - Outline of program - Vocabulary, technical terms
During	Learning guidance for: Storage, entry	- Participative exercise - Focussed viewing with checklists, questions Self-pacing with videotape: - Interspersed questions at end of sequences - Summaries - Cross-references to text - Selected note-taking tasks
After	Enhancing retention/retrieval	- Categorize material - Draw diagrams - Take short notes - Summarize—based on anchor images - Checklist of instructional objectives - Short summaries of program - Inference type questions
	Promoting transfer	- Analyze program using constructs in texts - Generalize/draw conclusions from TV material - Test, evaluate & compare how principles in text apply to real-world situations in TV - Discover relationships in TV material - Do further reading
	Eliciting performance	- Assignments for submission—testing skills developed in program - Assignments in correspondence texts based on programs - Self-assessment, self-remediation exercises - Application of TV material to other situations
Integration	Generalizations, conclusions Visual literacy skills	- Critical view of TV symbols & production aspects, producer's intent, effect of message - Intra-analysis—comparing and contrasting program segments - Inter-analysis—with other media - Self-directed projects related to TV material - Discussion groups at centers/Audioconferencing - Access to library resources
	Providing feedback	- Telephone diagnosis, remediation by instructor - Written comments on assignments - Computerized feedback - On-line computer communication/E-mail

program's information is absorbed. Each stage of television viewing is matched with the learning phases described by Gagne, and the instructional strategies and support described in the model are the "instructional events" that are designed to assist learning in each of these learning phases.

The initial concern in the "Before" stage of the model is to motivate the learner. Intrinsic motivation can be enhanced by presenting the learner with a set of goals/objectives of the television program. These goals must clearly delineate what they are supposed to learn from the program and which skills they are supposed to develop. If students are informed beforehand of the skills they should acquire, then assignments for submission which test these skills are justifiable. It is also very important at this stage to show the learners how the television program they are about to see relates to the rest of the course. Then, they will be made to see the "relevance" of the program to the aims and objectives of the course and the relationship to other course components.

The attention that has been aroused should then be directed so as to accomplish selective perception. Students should be given an indication of the nature of the television program—for instance, whether it presents an objective or subjective point of view, whether the material needs to be critically analyzed, whether it is an open-ended documentary format that can be interpreted, etc. Two or three points specifying what to look out for or discover in the program should be presented. It is important that these directions are kept short because short-term memory is limited in the amount of time and the number of items it can store.

Once the students' attention has been directed, it is crucial that they be given guidance for: (a) stimulating recall of necessary previously learned information, so that they can be helped to make associations, and (b) coding, storage and entry into long-term memory. Instructional strategies at this stage require the presentation of an advanced organizer and short directions to stimulate recognition of previous learning and recall of necessary propositions. Students can be given visual aids such as flow charts, or concept maps (a mapping technique), which impose some order on the material to be presented and help in categorizing the material after the presentation. Or, they could be furnished with diagrams, tables, and graphs, which may actually appear on the screen. Such visual material will help in the formation of concepts by providing concrete images and will also provide a means for revision of the television material later on. A short outline of the program can aid students organize the information, and a list of unfamiliar vocabulary to be encountered can allow them to learn the terms before watching the program.

While students are viewing the television program, guidance for storage and entry can be provided (a) by using a "participative exercise" which, for instance, requires the student to select during the program a correct feature illustrated in a text, or (b) by supplying checklists or questions which will focus their viewing. Activities at this stage should be kept to a minimum to allow for global viewing when the pace is continuous as in an open-broadcast delivery with no opportunity to record the material.

The survey results revealed that exercises requiring student responses during transmission were considered a very effective technique for integrating television presentations with the rest of the course. However, such a technique can be used effectively only if the television presentation is available in recorded form. Another effective method identified by the survey for helping students learn from television is screen presentation of the correct answer and discussion. Immediate knowledge of whether a student's response was accurate will enhance his or her learning. This technique, however, has to be built into the television script, or used by an instructor or tutor in Tutored Video Instruction (TVI).

If the television material is available on videocassettes, then self-pacing is possible. Students can be asked to stop the tape at the end of sequences, review the material, and respond to questions. They can be asked to take short notes, summarize, or complete an activity in the text or study guide based on the television material in a particular sequence.

Instructional strategies and support designed for the first step in the "After" stage are meant to enhance retention of what has been learned and to guarantee that "cues for retrieval" are available to the learner. The organization of television material into categories or in pictorial form—diagrams and tables provides a source of cues that serve to enhance later recall. Learning involves the formation of categories and coding systems. In order to remember something, it is sometimes sufficient to recall the coding system into which it falls. Students can be asked to take short notes and/or summarize information presented in the program, based on anchor images. Students can also be supplied with a checklist of instructional objectives, to determine whether they have learned the skills that they are supposed to have acquired. Short summaries of the program focusing on two or three main points will aid in later recall. Evaluation studies at the British Open University have indicated that providing a summary of the television program on an audiocassette with accompanying notes was considered very helpful by students.

Another technique is to ask students to respond to higher-level inference-type questions after viewing the program. Engaging in these follow-up activities will help the learner to acquire cognitive strategies for learning, remembering and thinking.

The second step of the "After" stage is to promote the transfer of learning. It is here that integration with the rest of the course components takes place. Students can be instructed to (a) analyze the real-world situation in the television program using theoretical concepts drawn from the text, (b) test, evaluate and compare how the principles in the text apply to the real-world situations in television, (c) discover relationships in the television material, (d) generalize or draw conclusions from the television material and figure out how insights gained can be applied to other situations, and (e) do further reading. These activities will help learners to acquire cognitive strategies which in turn will make them more capable of self-instruction.

The next step in the "After" stage is designed to elicit performance from students, which indicates to the instructor and students themselves how well they have learned the material and acquired the necessary skills. Performance is usually elicited in the form of assignments for submission. Assignments based on television programs can be inserted into study guides. These assignments could test the extent to which students can apply the television material to other situations. Self-assessment and self-remediation exercises can aid students in diagnosing their own problems and changing their learning to correct the perceived errors.

Instructional strategies and support designed for the next step of the "After" stage are meant to encourage the integration of the television experience. It is here that the program's information is integrated in the student's mind. Students are encouraged to undertake "holistic analysis" by drawing generalizations and conclusions, and to improve their visual literacy skills. The ideal support for this activity is the discussion group or "viewing group." Research has indicated that students are more likely to stop a videocassette which has been specially designed with clear stopping points and work through suggested activities in a group viewing situation rather than when working alone. This face-to-face interaction with a tutor and/or fellow students can occur at off-campus study centers.

Audioconferencing is a valuable support service for students at remote locations who cannot form a discussion group. Students linked by an audioconference bridge can discuss themes or ideas explored in the television program, and how they relate to information conveyed by other course components. Such discussions can enhance the development of information processing skills, and encourage learners to view television critically. Audioconferencing is an excellent means for interaction between the instructor and fellow students when the instructional delivery medium is noninteractive.

Activities at the integration stage which would enhance visual literacy skills or skills in using the medium involve: (a) a critical perception of the "language of television," television production techniques, the producer's intent, and the effect of the message; (b) intraanalysis—comparing and contrasting segments in the television presentation, and (c) interanalysis—comparing the effect of the television message with the effect of the messages delivered by other media. Visual literacy skills can be enhanced by providing students with information on media-based techniques—the variety of television formats and production techniques. Students can also be instructed at this stage to undertake self-directed projects based on the television material. In order for students to engage in further research it is necessary to ensure access to library resources.

The various activities designed for the "After" stage should take into account the different cognitive styles in adult learners. They can also aid the development of certain cognitive styles; encourage field-dependents to engage in holistic analysis and convergers to engage in divergent thinking.

The next important step is feedback to students. Telephone office hours or a 24-hour hotline can be open for students to clarify problems regarding the television program. On-line computer communication would be desirable if available. Written comments on assignments based on the television material and/or computerized feedback would help students to consolidate their learning. These comments should be explanatory rather than judgmental. For some learning outcomes, such as cognitive strategies, the feedback must convey the degree to which the learner's performance approaches some standard. It is also important to keep in mind the usefulness of frequent and immediate feedback during the acquisition of newly learned capabilities.

The ultimate purpose of the model is to enable learners to develop cognitive strategies: strategies for attending, learning, remembering, and thinking. It is hoped that the instructional strategies and support systems described in the model will aid in the achievement of this goal. It has become evident from the review of literature and the survey results that activities should be designed for students to engage in *before* and *after* they view the television presentation if effective learning is to take place.

A study guide can describe how the video component relates to textual and other material in that course and to the overall objectives of the course. If the distance teaching institution produces its own television programs, correspondence texts, audiocassettes, and other material, then the integration techniques and cross-references to other course material can be built in. If preproduced television programs are leased from other institutions, the study guide should include the instructional strategies described in the model suitable for that learning situation. Study guides are most useful to students when they describe the relationship between the television programs and the texts.

The model aims to show that effective learning from a television component in a distance-study course can take place if the necessary instructional strategies and support services are provided.

Instructional television programs are more likely to be effective when they are one component of a multimedia package, than when they are used on their own without supporting materials. The model was also designed to help institutions that were not producing their own television programs.

It must be emphasized that the model describes an ideal situation and that all the strategies described for each learning phase need not be used. The model delineates possible strategies that will aid learning in each phase. These strategies and support systems have to be selected within the context of the constraints of the distance teaching institution's organizational characteristics and the characteristics of the adult learner for whom the instruction is designed. It might be necessary to modify the techniques described to suit the individual learning styles of a specific student population.

One limitation of the model is that it presents a highly structured approach to television viewing. Autonomous learners who do not like structure imposed on instructional materials, may reject the guidance and direction. The model, however, was developed on the assumption that not all adult students are self-directed inquirers, and that some of them require "learning-how-to-learn" activities.

CONCLUSION

The integration of video-based technologies into distance education programs poses significant challenges to educators. Too often technologies are selected because of their sophisticated capabilities or their popular appeal without considering either their educational capabilities or their effect on teaching and learning.

Adopting a technology for delivering instruction, requires careful consideration of not only how it will fit instructional needs and learner characteristics, but also to what extent it will need additional support systems to make the teaching learning process effective. Student support services and instructional strategies that can facilitate learning in a distance teaching system should be integrated with the medium of instructional delivery.

The consequence of careless adoption of a technological solution may contribute to the failure of distance education programs. This can be avoided if ample attention is paid not only to how well the instructional technology fits learner characteristics and instructional needs but also to the extent to which student support services and instructional strategies are integrated into the planning and implementation of distance education.

REFERENCES

Bates, A. W. (1983). Adult Learning from Educational Television: The Open University Experience. In M. J. A. Howe (Ed.), *Learning from Television: Psychological and Educational Research*. London: Academic Press.

Bates, A. W. (1987). *Television, Learning and Distance Education*. IET Paper No. 262. Milton Keynes, U.K.: The Open University, Institute of Educational Technology.

Bates, T. (1984). Broadcast Television in Distance Education: A World-Wide Perspective. In A. W. Bates (Ed.), *The Role of Technology in Distance Education*. London: Croom Helm.

Gagne, R. M. (1977). *The Conditions of Learning* (3rd ed.). New York: Holt, Rinehart and Winston.

Gunawardena, C. N. (1988). New Communications Technologies and Distance Education: A Paradigm for the Integration of Video-Based Instruction." Unpublished doctoral dissertation, Department of Curriculum and Instruction, University of Kansas.

Hodgson, V. E. (1986). The Interrelationship Between Support and Learning Materials." *Programmed Learning and Educational Technology, 23* (1), 56–61.

Holmberg, B. (1981). *Status and Trends of Distance Education*. London: Kogan Page.

Waniewicz, I. (1972). *Broadcasting for Adult Education: A Guide Book to World-Wide Experience*. Switzerland UNESCO.

Willen, B. (1988). What Happened to the Open University: Briefly. *Distance Education, 9,* 71–83.

Wohl, A., and Tidhar, C. E. (1988, January). Learning to View—Viewing to Learn: A Macro and Micro Integrative Teaching System of Television Viewing. *TechTrends, 33,* 12–16.

CHAPTER 10

A NEW FRAMEWORK AND PERSPECTIVE

D. Randy Garrison and Doug Shale

In our view it is unfortunate that some systems are expending vast amounts of time and money trying to devise learning packages which will allow students to become completely independent of teachers and other students. In these systems the notion of learning as a social experience has not received the consideration we believe it warrants. (Smith & Small, 1982, p. 139)

Throughout this book we have emphasized the process issues of distance education and have attempted to integrate them with the more obvious and historically predominant structural features. Education, be it face-to-face or at a distance, is more than packaging content and the uncritical assimilation of that content. The transaction between teacher and student is at the heart of the educational process and distance educators must address this reality when attempting to overcome the constraints of distance. The issues of designing instruction at a distance are complex given the range of existing and emerging technologies as well as content, student and instructional demands. However, the one thing to be certain of is that the quality and effectiveness of education at a distance is directly attributable to the degree and kind of interaction between teacher and student, as well as between student and student.

In this chapter we address ourselves more widely to a selected set of issues that we feel will be the focus of future discussions of distance education. Much of the concern is with communication needs in the distance education transaction. Another, more specific matter, which is one of the fundamental concerns of distance educators, is the issue of "independence" and its worthiness as a goal in itself. Other issues have to do with the effectiveness and quality of the educational transaction at a distance as well as with distance education's relationship with the field of education in general.

INDEPENDENCE

As we indicated earlier, a lot of effort has been devoted to justifying distance education as a unique form of learning and one of the major characteristics used to justify the uniqueness of distance education is the students' independence. An independence, we might add, that was created by the necessity of study at a distance through print and mail communication. When independence as individual physical isolation was no longer a necessary consequence of studying at a distance due to the new communications technology, some distance educators began to question the distinction made between conventional and distance education (Sewart, 1981, 1982; Smith & Kelly, 1987).

Holmberg (1987) observed that in North America independent study often appears to be a synonym for distance education. He proceeded to suggest that if "distance is seen as conducive to autonomy this could be interpreted as regarding dialogue as at variance with student autonomy" (Holmberg, 1987, p. 4). While Holmberg suggests this is inaccurate, it does describe a bias of many distance educators who assume all distance education students are autonomous. More importantly, however, it inflates and distorts the importance of this concept. Education is a social process and as Chene (1983) states, we must not "forget that knowledge and skill competency are social products" (p. 46). The concept of independence as individual isolation is clearly at odds with this view of education.

The dilemma of independence in distance education has often been stated in the form of two positions. The first suggests that students are and want to be independent (which is why they choose distance education). The second believes they should be helped to become more independent (Holmberg, 1987). Unfortunately, this really begs the question of whether autonomy is desirable, realistic, or even possible to attain. It has been argued by Garrison (1989) that this concept of independence is ambiguous and by itself is rather a simplistic notion. Considering the complexity of the educational enterprise the usual notion of independence runs a serious risk of obscuring the true nature of education. The concept of independence does not provide a guiding educational philosophy and, therefore, we need to look for something more.

It has been proposed by Garrison (1989) and Garrison and Baynton (1987) that the educational transaction can be viewed on two levels. At the macro-level we have the common description of education in terms of three components—teacher, student, and content. However, the model proposed by these authors goes beyond this largely morphological conceptualization to consider specifically various process elements in the educational transaction. They suggest that at the micro-level the transaction is influenced by the elements of independence (freedom to choose goals), proficiency (ability and motivation to learn), and support (human and nonhuman resources) which together constitute true control of the educational transaction. Control, therefore, may be defined as the opportunity and ability to direct the course of educational activities.

The key to this model is that the two overlapping triadic relationships be in dynamic balance and balance can only be realized through sustained two-way communication between teacher and student. Communication should be facilitated at two distinct stages in distance education. The first is the planning stage largely concerned with the macro-level considerations of the model. In distance education (as well as much of conventional education) this is usually nonexistent. The second stage of communication is the instructional process which represents a shift to the control elements of the model at the micro-level. Independence is only one of a number of factors to be considered in an educational transaction.

The point is that control, as defined previously, is a more useful concept than independence in understanding and planning for education at a distance. In addition, the concept of control also emphasizes the crucial role that communication plays in establishing an appropriate balance of the various components of the educational transaction. Clearly distance education is more than simply providing a professionally packaged set of materials. Unfortunately, though as Sewart (1987) suggests, "the individual needs of the student learning alone and at a distance has often become lost in the overriding requirement to produce a grandiose package of materials" (p. 33).

Teaching is an essential component of an educational enterprise. Teaching, however, is not just producing and transmitting course content. A teacher is more than an information resource and an arranger of the educational environment. The emphasis on education as a collaborative process is not just to ensure voluntariness on the part of the learner but, more importantly, to ensure the integration of social and personal knowledge by challenging existing views and considering alternative perspectives. As Jarvis (1988) points out, it is very difficult for individuals to become critically aware and develop insights into their own condition through independent self-reflection since they are largely constrained by their previous socialization. The educational process is dependent upon sustained dialogue and negotiation between teacher and student.

Howard's (1987) view that the "quality of feedback given to students studying at a distance is likely to be of critical importance to their experience as learners and to the outcomes of that experience" (p. 24) under-

scores the importance of two-way communication. The evidence in support of this statement can be found in the general discussions around the
educational transaction and good pedagogy as well as in the statistics
concerning persistence. Dropout in distance education has often been
associated with a sense of social and academic isolation (Garrison, 1987;
Sweet, 1986). In addition, students themselves rate highly the usefulness
of learning activities that help overcome difficulties with the learning
package (Kember & Dekkers, 1987).

Winn states in Chapter 5, that "distance education need not depart
from the principles of good pedagogy simply because of the constraints
imposed by the circumstances." Learning independently through a mass
produced package of information does not ensure the acquisition and
validation of knowledge. As we have attempted to emphasize in this
book, good pedagogy and the integrity of the educational process are
dependent upon mediation. To paraphrase Sewart (1982), the requirement of mediation (two-way communication) does not contradict the
essence of distance education; and if it appears to, then the fault lies in
the overly simplistic concept of distance education.

ACCESS AND QUALITY ASSURANCE

With recent developments in communications technology problems in
accessing relevant information will soon become a nonissue. Since the
advent of correspondence education, great strides have been made to
provide access to information and learning for the vast majority of the
literate population. More recent advances have used broadcast radio
and television to expand the range of coded information (i.e., symbol
systems). Now with the recent proliferation of computers, extensive
databases, and laser discs, access to vast quantities of information is
readily available to a majority of the population. However, as important
and necessary as it is to access information, it is only one aspect of the
educational picture. As we have noted repeatedly, the viability and
success of an educational endeavor is dependent upon providing adequate support.

Moore (1987) in an article focusing on the distance learner, states that
there is an acute danger in distance education of overemphasizing the
dissemination of information. He goes on to suggest that the learner is
looking for at least five qualities in the distance education program. The
learners expect: (1) to have communicated to them a body of knowledge; (2) the body of presented knowledge to be accompanied by guidance; (3) to do something with the knowledge; (4) to have feedback

from their activities; and (5) to have assistance in dealing with unexpected problems (Moore, 1987, pp. 61–62). Clearly the learner expects that a distance education experience goes beyond simple access to information or societal knowledge. From a programming perspective, Moore (1987) goes on to say that he believes "maximum ingenuity should be applied to establishing learner systems to give individual support locally to those who learn through distance mediums" (p. 63).

Support in the sense that Moore uses the term goes beyond one-way access to information and physical resources. It suggests various forms of interaction of the student with a teacher/tutor. Such issues of interaction take us beyond independence and the structural aspects of distance education. Interaction and dialogue make it possible to offer new perspectives, explanatory feedback, and to validate knowledge as well as to provide opportunities for external areas of support. Issues surrounding interaction and communication address effectiveness and quality concerns regarding the educational process. Without two-way communication and opportunities for meaningful dialogue it is unlikely that the cognitive aspects of the educational process will be addressed in a quality manner.

Access to education and quality assurance of learning have also been discussed by Ehrmann (1988) from a communications technology perspective. He suggests that the more problems students have with access, the more extensively institutions appear to rely on a materials transport strategy. Ehrmann (1988) then questions whether this is sufficient and states:

> Transmitting materials to students, even materials such as computer-based tools and databases, implies that the instruction can be transported whole from the instructor's head into the student's. But few faculty would see an implantation of their own ideas into students as liberal learning. Instead they want students to become engaged in personally thinking *about* the materials, to develop their own sense of the tools, resources, and findings of the field, and how to use them. That means that the student somehow has to learn to take command, actively posing and solving problems, screening for appropriate information, experimenting with tools, and in the process developing a deep understanding of the possibilities and limits of the field. (p. 5)

Ehrmann (1988) believes as we do that, without dialogue or conversation, quality learning seems less likely. He states, "Without rich opportunities for such conversations it is hard to imagine a student really learning to engage sophisticated materials, or even to understand the deeper meaning of what a professor has just said" (Ehrmann, 1988, p. 7). However, the question that needs to be addressed is what is the nature of these conversations and can the new technologies facilitate such conversations between teacher and student. Ehrmann (1988) believes that both accessibility and quality learning can be achieved with new communications technology and these technologies are capable of supporting three classic types of academic conversation. These are:

1. the creative, interactive use of the tools, resources, and didactic materials of the field;
2. timely (instantaneous) conversation about what is being learned with the faculty and other students; and
3. time-delayed conversation about what is being learned, through the exchange of homework and projects, and the receipt of feedback. (Ehrmann, 1988, p. 1)

It is important to stress the interdependent nature of the three types of academic conversation. Unfortunately, distance educators have largely relied upon the first type of conversation.

While there is much that could be elaborated upon regarding Ehrmann's discussion of technologies for access and quality, three points are directly applicable to the theme of this book. First, quality educational transactions are dependent upon two-way communication where both sender and receiver are changed by the conversation. This, of course reinforces what has been said in previous chapters. Second, we are given a clearer appreciation of the types of conversation required in an educational setting whether it is at a distance or face-to-face. Third, it should be encouraging and enlightening to distance educators that we have the technology to enable these important kinds of conversation between teacher and student as well as between student and student.

Further to the issue of quality being associated with two-way communication, there would appear to be a relationship between interactive capabilities and persistence in a distance education course or program. Is it a coincidence that completion rates increase as we move from exclusively home study materials, to home study materials with a tutor available, to home study materials with teleconferencing where students may interact with other students (Garrison, 1987)? While there are many factors which influence dropout in education, it is argued here that improving the quality of the educational process through increased two-way communication is likely to have the most significant impact upon the effectiveness of learning and in turn is likely to raise completion rates in distance education. To this point there has been a lot of discussion regarding teacher-student interaction but little has been said of the value and problems of encouraging and facilitating student-student interaction. We turn to this point in the next section.

SOCIAL INTERACTION

While it is clear that, broadly speaking, education is a social activity, there is some question whether distance education should consider the more specific social needs of students interacting with other students. In conventional education students are often the greatest support for other students. Not only can they provide academic support and opportunities to validate knowledge but students may also provide invaluable counselling beyond purely academic matters to other students. The question is, "How essential are other students in the educational process?"

In adult education the social aspects of learning have always been given considerable prominence and we must appreciate that a large number of distance education students are adult learners. Houle's (1961) seminal study of the motivational orientations of adult learners revealed multiple and overlapping motives for learning. Adult students were seen as goal, activity, and learning oriented. Subsequent psychometric research has confirmed Houle's typology although additional categories or subcategories have been added. All of these typologies, however, have a social dimension to them. That is, adults participate in learning for social (activity) reasons as well as for instrumental reasons or cognitive interest. Therefore, distance educators should address not only cognitive learning but also social needs. To ignore the social dimension of learning is to artificially separate the functions of learning and living. As distance educators we have the means to integrate learning and living for the adult to a greater extent than we have seen to date.

One approach to education at a distance capable of addressing both the cognitive and social dimensions deserving special attention is the local study center. It has been suggested by others that local study centers may have a role, but extensive use of study centers contradicts the basic premise of distance education. Our position is that independence is not an essential characteristic of distance education and, therefore, study centers do not inherently contradict this form of education. Decisions about the appropriateness of technology will depend upon a number of factors associated with the educational transaction. For example, dismissing extensive use of study centers would effectively eliminate education at a distance that largely relies on the group dynamics of teleconferencing since such methods generally require students to travel to local centers.

Study centers support a variety of functions related to academic and administrative issues. The functions of a study center have been described by Sewart (1987) as follows:

> In some it has been seen as a viewing centre where replay devices may be used. In others it has been seen as a library resource centre. In some it has been seen as the focus for student interaction and self-help groups, a substitute for the conventional campus. In yet others it has been offered as a site for practical experiments or the use of equipment, such as computing facilities, which are essential to study but which cannot be offered easily to the student at home. Finally, there are cases where study centres are valued as a tangible link between the otherwise impersonal distance teaching institution and the local community. (p. 34)

While study centers certainly provide an opportunity for social contact and face-to-face tuition, they can and do provide much more. For some programs, study centers may be the only realistic means for supporting the educational transaction and achieving the desired educational goals. However, as noted in Chapter 4, perhaps one of the more essential purposes of the study center, given the increased use of sophisticated technology, may be to provide equitable access to new technological delivery systems for those members of society who might otherwise be deprived of educational opportunities.

CONVERGENCE

Increasingly we are finding less reason to maintain and promote a sharp distinction between conventional and distance education methods. Both in theory and in practice the distinction is becoming untenable. Philosophically, it cannot be justified that distance education is essentially different from conventional educational methods. The physical separation of teacher and student is a relatively minor constraint that can be and is being addressed in a variety of ways with existing and emerging communications technology. To see only the differences between conventional and distance education is to restrict the growth of distance education and its capability to equitably meet the needs of all potential students. While we defend the essential nature of the educational transaction, we emphasize that we are not apologists for conventional methods which are too often authoritarian systems focused upon an unquestioning acceptance of subject content.

The principles and rationale of higher distance education are essentially those of adult education. Adults are the primary audience we serve and the methods we have adopted have historically respected the voluntariness of adult learning. The foundation of adult education is interdependence and collaboration between teacher and student as well as the integration of learning with the everyday roles and responsibilities of adult life. The challenge accepted by adult education to reach out to all would-be learners is considerable. However, distance education methods together with existing conventional systems will converge for the benefit of all learners—not just those we define as adults.

As Jevons points out in the final chapter, distance education students are not so different from campus-based students. In fact, given the current interest in the "andragogical" approach by the educational community in general, we are beginning to see that education is more than information giving. While authority is certainly a legitimate part of the educational transaction, authoritarian and coercive methods violate the integrity of the transaction. Therefore, although distance education methods may have adopted the principles of adult education, this does not exclude students based solely on age as a criterion.

The blurring of the boundaries between distance education and conventional education represents a convergence of the two approaches. Eventually this may result in increasingly "open" educational systems. Foks (1987b), among others, has argued that we should do away with the notions of "on-campus" and "off-campus" in favor of an open learning approach. Such an approach would cause us to think in terms of a range of strategies and resources most appropriate for each student. According to Foks (1987b), strategies "will differ according to degree and nature of student-teacher interaction" . . . [and for] any of these strategies a choice of resources has to be made" (p. 37). Open learning systems address both access (resources) and support (educational strategies) components of learning.

A view of open learning relevant to this book is provided by Harris (1988). He suggests that open learning as generally discussed in the literature is concerned with "the amount and type of learner choice in the system" (p. 13), but what is missed is a critical analysis of what "learner choice" really means. For example, an over reliance on prepackaged materials is a problem because such materials may oversimplify arguments and prematurely dismiss conflicting viewpoints. On the other hand, ironically, too much emphasis on learner "center-ness" and independence may build in closure. As Harris (1988) states, "it is becoming clear that more attention needs to be given to what learners actually do with the material once they receive it in distance systems too: we can no longer assume that learners set out simply to reproduce the arguments in the materials" (p. 15). The lines of communication must be opened and we must be vigilant that independence not lead to uncritical analysis of content and closure in an insidious manner.

Open learning systems are concerned with choice and control. Through the resulting flexibility of provision (i.e., communications technology) various geographical, socioeconomic and psychological barriers are reduced. Choice, like freedom, must be exercised with responsibility and awareness of the nature of the educational transaction. Choice or access to information resources does not ensure that educationally worthwhile goals will be identified or achieved. Control as defined previously in a broad educational context will ensure that appropriate support and academic discourse are provided. An open learning system does not encourage freedom of choice for the learner acting in isolation.

While distance education methods provide necessary and important strategies for the development of open learning systems, the two are not synonymous. The point has been made several times previously that education at a distance is not some unique form of learning. Just as it will serve little purpose to artificially separate distance education from conventional education, it should matter little how we categorize methods and strategies in open learning systems. The key features of educational systems of the future will be choice and control within the confines of a balanced educational transaction. Distance and adult educators are pioneering the development of truly open and integrated delivery systems but the evidence of their success may well be the demise of adult and distance education as nascent disciplines or even distinct fields of practice. Instead we will come to view educational transactions from a more integrated and holistic perspective.

Distance education methods provide important alternative strategies for the facilitation of the educational transaction. While distance education represents a break from conventional thinking about educational provision, it too represents a different kind of closure with regard to academic discourse that must be addressed. It has been argued by Harris (1988) that open learning in the Open University tradition, with its technological preoccupation with the learning package, needs to break with old conceptions and practices. Established practices and contexts block thinking and "new moves to openness can indicate at best a process of changing from one pole to another, but without changing the framework. Despite the promise of a radical departure from existing practice, in the name of liberating the learner, there is a risk of merely modernising existing practice and subjecting the learner to more rational and individualised controls" (Harris, 1988, p. 14).

We have attempted to demonstrate throughout this book that education is more than simply transmitting information. There is a need in distance education for a new framework and perspective that recognizes the necessity of dialogue and academic discourse to acquire knowledge. The perspectives on distance education presented in each of the chapters have attempted to recognize the need not only for access to (i.e., choice) but support of (i.e., control) the educational process through various modes of communication. The time is right to establish a new vision in distance education; a vision not confined to past practice. From an appreciation of education in its best form and with the means of existing and emerging communications technology we can begin to approximate that vision. The challenge is to preserve (restore?) the integrity of the educational transaction through appropriate sustained dialogue between teacher and student. In short, we need to view distance education more as education at a distance.

REFERENCES

Chene, A. (1983). The Concept of Autonomy in Adult Education: A Philosophical Discussion. *Adult Education Quarterly, 34*, 38–47.

Ehrmann, S. C. (1988). *Technologies for Access and Quality: An Agenda for Three Conversations.* Washington, D.C.: Annenberg/CPB Project.

Foks, J. Towards Open Learning. (1987a). In P. Smith and M. Kelly (Eds.), *Distance Education and the Mainstream* (pp. 74–92). London: Croom Helm.

Foks, J. (1987b). Will the Walls Come Tumbling Down? *International Council for Distance Education Bulletin, 3,* 35–40.

Garrison, D. R. (1987). Researching Dropout in Distance Education. *Distance Education, 8,* 95–101.

Garrison, D. R. (1989). *Understanding Distance Education: A Framework for the Future.* London: Routledge.

Garrison, D. R. & Baynton, M. (1987). Beyond Independence in Distance Education: The Concept of Control. *The American Journal of Distance Education, 1*(3), 3–15.

Harris, D. (1988). The Micro-politics of Openness. *Open Learning, 3*(2), 13–16.

Holmberg, B. (1987). Student Autonomy in Theory and Practice. *International Journal of Innovative Higher Education, 4*(1/2), 4–8.

Houle, C. O. (1961). The Inquiring Mind. Madison: University of Wisconsin Press.

Howard, D. C. (1987). Designing Learner Feedback in Distance Education. *The American Journal of Distance Education, 1*(3), 24–40.

Jarvis, P. (1988). Needs, Interests, and Adult Learning. *Transatlantic Dialogue:*

A Research Exchange, Leeds: University of Leeds, School of Continuing Education, 200–205.

Kember, D., & Dekkers, J. (1987). The Role of Study Centres for Academic Suport in Distance Education. *Distance Education, 8*(1), 4–17.

Moore, M. G. (1987), Learners and Learning at a Distance. *International Council for Distance Education Bulletin, 14,* 59–65.

Sewart, D. (1981). Distance Teaching: A Contradiction in Terms? *Teaching at a Distance, 19,* 8–18.

Sewart, D. (1982). Individualizing Support Services. In J. S. Daniel, M. A. Stroud and J. R. Thompson (Eds.), *Learning at a Distance: A World Perspective.* Edmonton: Athabasca University.

Sewart, D. (1987). Limitations of the Learning Package. In M. Thorpe and D. Grugeon (Eds.), *Open Learning for Adults.* Burnt Mill, UK: Longman House.

Smith, P., & Kelly, M. (1987). *Distance Education and the Mainstream.* London: Croom Helm.

Smith, K. C., & Small, I. W. (1982). Student Support: How Much is Enough. In J. S. Daniel, M. A. Stroud and J. R. Thompson (Eds.), *Learning at a Distance: A World Perspective.* Edmonton: Athabasca University.

Sweet, R. (1986). Student Dropout in Distance Education: An Application of Tinto's Model. *Distance Education, 7*(2), 201–213.

CHAPTER 11

BLURRING THE BOUNDARIES: PARITY AND CONVERGENCE

Fred Jevons

In earlier writings (Jevons, 1982, 1984) I have advanced the thesis that distance education deserves to be accorded a "parity of esteem" with the conventional face-to-face mode of instruction. I argued that "Distance education is no longer a makeshift second best to be used only where the face-to-face mode is geographically impossible" (Jevons, 1984, p. 24), and "One should not be too much on the defensive about distance education" (p. 32). The basis of my argument was that, while "distance education will come off second best if it is compared with a romanticised picture of a traditional university" (pp. 31–32), it has a number of intrinsically educational advantages and, as a result, deserves parity of esteem.

I will go into these later in the chapter, but the theme I wished to develop was that, in some circumstances, the merits of distance education lead naturally to its being the preferred mode of study. I argued for a parity of esteem because it seemed to me that distance education was often dismissed on grounds of prejudice, without due consideration for its potential ". . . as a leading edge in a movement for more flexible designs in learning in general" (Jevons, 1984, p. 25).

I had also suggested that as distance education gained a parity of esteem and overcame the prejudices against it, we would see a convergence of distance education and campus-based education with respect to the methods they use and the clienteles they serve. In other words, the boundaries distinguishing these modes of education are becoming blurred. However, if there are boundaries that are being blurred, it is of interest to inquire into why the boundaries were there in the first place. In this chapter I consider boundaries based on four factors: first, the age of the clientele; second, the quality (real and perceived) of provision; third, the question of cost; and fourth, the meaning of "distance" in distance education.

My answers are to some extent unconventional ones. Extrapolating the trends that are blurring the boundaries, I conclude that the outcomes could be highly desirable.

THE AGE OF THE CLIENTELE

Distance education has been set apart from traditional face-to-face education by a number of factors. One of them is age.

I came to the practice of distance education with a package of pre-suppositions derived from the UK Open University (OU). I make no apology for this. The success of the OU in the early 1970s was striking. The new institution had instant charisma. People soon came to claim it as a mark of distinction *not* to have been to Milton Keynes to visit the headquarters from which tens of thousands of students were served. If the OU said that distance education is for adults, that just had to be right, and it was some years before I came to question this near dogma.

Nothing I say here should be taken to detract from the OU's achievement. I still regard it as one of the greatest educational innovations of the century. I had been appointed in 1975 as Foundation Vice Chancellor of Deakin University in Australia, and I was determined to take the distance education mission of my new university seriously. The OU was for me the shining model to emulate. Before I left the UK for Australia I looked around the UK universities and polytechnics for interesting new developments and usually it turned out to be the OU where the most exciting things were happening.

That success of the OU is in itself part of the point I am trying to make. The OU was born into an environment in which the UK universities had largely phased out part-time degrees. The visitors who came from the OU to Deakin in the late 70s sometimes had to be reminded that there are ways other than distance education by which an adult can study for a degree. In Australia, by contrast with the UK situation, there remained a substantial population of adult students in the traditional universities. Conversely some—not much, but some—of the distance education provision by Australian higher education institutions was for school leavers.

I agree that some of the best applications of distance education are for adults. Mid-career education is particularly appropriate for this mode. But nothing I have found in the literature on "andragogy" supports a sharp separation of clientele by age. Much of the strength of the myth that associates distance education particularly and uniquely with an adult clientele derives, I believe, from a historically contingent circumstance—the near absence of other provision for degree level education for adults in the UK at the time that the OU was born.

The point was brought home to me forcefully at the conference organized by the OU in 1979 on the education of adults at a distance. I took with me to Birmingham a paper which asked "how different is the distance student?" (Jevons, 1979). I thought I might be able to generate some interesting discussion by putting the unorthodox view that distance education students are not so very different from campus-based students.

My hope was not fulfilled. My argument was not disputed—it was just ignored. People didn't want to know. Only in retrospect does the explanation become clear to me. The OU's interest was in carving out a distinctive role for itself. OU staff claimed to be doing a different job for a different category of students. Their very existence depended on the difference. For the many clones of the OU from around the world who also flocked to the conference, the same article of faith supplied a similar institutional role and identity and justification.

There had, it is true, been a pilot scheme for younger students. Launched in the early days of the OU, it was at best an equivocal success (Woodley and MacIntosh, 1980). The conclusion was that distance education is not suitable for school leavers, or at least that school leavers require a different and more generous support system to achieve success rates comparable to those of adult OU students.

So great was the charisma of the OU that a pragmatic, country specific and historically specific decision almost became a worldwide dogma.

There was an enticing neatness about the concept: distance education for adults, campus-based education for school leavers. But the factual basis for it was thin. And there was something strange about the argument. In many developing countries, in Africa for instance, the distance education mode is used to provide a major part of secondary education. Even in Australia there are well established correspondence schools offering secondary level education. It was difficult to understand why distance education should not be suitable for an intermediate age range when it can demonstrably be made to work for both younger and older students.

So that was one previously sharp boundary that for me became blurred, and I believe a more general recognition of this blurring is important. As was accurately foreseen by Anwyl, Powles and Patrick (1986), the question of the suitability for school leavers of distance education, or at least some aspects of it, urgently needs to be reexamined. There may be some techniques of distance education which are particularly applicable to this group and the loosening of institutional constraints may be particularly welcome to them.

The difficulties are attitudinal rather than technical. I believe academic staff would do well to consider more sympathetically new work practices which, in the light of new possibilities created by modern technology, could with advantage replace some of the time honored conventions of the educational system. Staff/student ratios are no longer a satisfactory indicator of the quality of provision. In a modern car factory, quality is not adequately measured by the number of employees per car produced. Metal workers seem more ready these days than some academics and educational administrators to consider radical changes in the mode of production.

This line of argument raises three new sets of questions: The relative quality of provision, real and perceived, that traditional and modern techniques offer; their relative costs; and the meaning of "distance" in distance education. I will take up each of these in turn.

QUALITY OF PROVISION

If the "second best" image is firmly imprinted on distance education, the reason is understandable, but it is historical rather than grounded in present fact. Distance education was first introduced for situations where traditional face-to-face education was impossible. Now, I believe, distance education deserves to be treated with parity of esteem.

The onus of proof is, as usual, on the new. The old is accepted without question. Often, I have found, even experienced educators, who are well aware of what is or can be wrong with traditional education, forget all about that when it comes to comparing it with distance education. Inevitably distance education will come off second best if it is compared with a rosily nostalgic view of campus-based education in which there is never a timetable clash to restrict subject choice; in which no student and no teacher ever has an illness or a family crisis; in which every student participates eagerly in tutorials, and avidly discusses work with other students late into the night; in which all teachers are in complete command over everything they teach and are adept in every pedagogic strategy and ruse. I have repeatedly asked, "if such a university exists, will someone please tell me where it is?" (Jevons, 1984, 1987). So far I have had no response.

My argument is that distance education has advantages as well as disadvantages as compared with campus-based education. In comparing the two modes, therefore, it is misleading to ask simply which is better. The question should be, better for what, and in what circumstances?

Let me be specific. I see six types of advantage in distance education. First and most obvious, it provides easier access for many people. It offers greater flexibility and eases constraints of timing and location. Barriers to campus-based education such as geographical isolation, family commitments and the requirements of employment are lower.

Second, because of their separation from the teacher, distance education students approach more closely the ideal of the autonomous learner. Of course they do not always learn idependently in practice, but it can be argued that the circumstances are more conducive for them to do so.

Third, students who have jobs do not have to leave them to study by distance education. There is less disjunction, therefore, between the context of work and the context of study and it is easier for students to relate the one to the other. Distance education shares this advantage with part-time campus-based education, but for this mode the geographic constraint is tight. You cannot be a part-time campus-based student unless you are within easy reach of a campus.

Fourth, quality control is better. Even in the best campus-based institutions there are some lectures and some tutorials which are not as good as they might be. It is different in distance education. The materials that are used in distance education are in the public domain and available for scrutiny by everybody. A lecturer's words vanish into thin air within an instant, but distance education materials have an enduring existence, unfailingly consistent week after week.

Fifth, there is an opportunity for cumulative improvement in pedagogic quality. This follows from quality control. Because the materials are in the public domain they are subject to criticism and open to improvement through criticism.

Sixth, there is a staff development effect. This is another consequence of quality control. When you know that you are going to appear in print it concentrates the mind wonderfully!

Consequently, a different pattern of advantages and disadvantages exists in distance education as compared with traditional campus-based education. Which is "better" depends on the circumstances and the requirements of any particular situation.

THE QUESTION OF COST

In the early days of Deakin University politicians and administrators often used to ask me whether distance education is cheaper. I came to anticipate the look of disapproval on their faces when I began my answer with "well it depends on. . . ." That is just the sort of answer that politicians and administrators do not like to get.

But the trouble is that it does depend! It depends very much on the circumstances and the requirements of a particular situation.

Distance education is not homogeneous. It encompasses a great range of possible techniques—indeed that is its hallmark. It shows a greater readiness to use alternative techniques of delivery. The cost depends on what mix of techniques is chosen, on the nature and scatter of the population to be served, and on the number of students in the system. Distance education systems are characterized by bigger up front costs because good materials are expensive to develop. Above all, the cost depends on the richness of the support system that is provided.

Estimates have been made of the size at which distance education becomes more cost effective than traditional education. Thus Keegan and Rumble (1982) estimated that it is in the range 9,000 to 22,000 students that an institution becomes more cost effective. In Australia the Commonwealth Tertiary Education Commission (1986, p. 227) has made a "per subject" estimate based on enrolments in a subject. In the conditions of a typical Australian college of advanced education it suggested that distance education becomes cost effective when enrolments in a subject are above a threshold which lies between 50 and 150.

In neither case, I'm sure, would anybody wish to pretend that these figures are anything other than rubbery.

It is understandable that distance educators have been criticized for producing so few figures, but in practical terms it really is not a very meaningful calculation to make. In practice a distance education institution does the best it can with the dollars it has. A better question would be, what standard of materials and support services do you achieve given the dollars that you spend? That question unfortunately is rarely asked.

One clear point is that "selling" distance education on the basis of cheapness is a two edged sword. If the system once established has to be run inexpensively, the quality of the materials and the richness of student support are bound to suffer.

THE MEANING OF DISTANCE

Those who were fortunate enough to attend the World Congress on Distance Education in Vancouver in 1982 will remember the debate on whether the name of the international council should be changed from correspondence education to distance education. Distance education won, but it is not without drawbacks. The word distance tends to suggest that distance education is only or mainly for people who are geographically isolated, separated by large distances from educational institutions.

This time the presupposition is more an Australian than a British one. Distance education in Australia was originally intended to serve the outback. Some Australian institutions as recently as a few years ago prohibited local students from studying "externally." This ban naturally led to the formation of a black market in distance education materials. Deakin University was, to the best of my knowledge, the first to consciously plan to use distance education materials for on-campus teaching. It turned the black market into an official policy.

With the growth of the "open learning" movement (Foks, 1987), other aspects of openness have become disassociated from the element of distance. Thus a further blurring of boundaries has occurred. The respective clienteles are now merged by geography as well as by age.

ADVANTAGES OF BLURRING THE BOUNDARIES

The old argument of single versus dual mode institutions is now back in the melting pot. There can be no doubt that some of the most significant advances in distance education have been made by single mode institutions: notably by the Open University in the UK and its clones in other countries, and by institutions such as the Open Learning Agency in British Columbia. We should take care not to forget the lessons that have been learned by institutions such as these. The word is getting around now that there is no great mystique about distance education. This together with severe pressures on public funding, is leading to a tendency to scrap the purpose-built mechanisms created to serve this particular group of students. It is being suggested that traditional institutions can quite easily serve this special group as a minor add-on to their mainstream activities (Campion & Kelly, 1988). If that happens it will be a reversion to the pre-1970 situation in which these students were not well served.

There is a real danger here of a loss of quality of the materials and a watering down of the support systems which genuine distance education students need. The translating machine may have been righter than it knew when it translated "out of sight, out of mind" into "invisible maniac."

But there are also some advantages that can come from a deliberate blurring of the boundaries between pure distance education and pure traditional campus based education. They concern both quality and cost.

The possibility that campus-based teaching may be improved by the more rigorous requirements of distance teaching is discussed by Smith (1987). There can be a sort of "technology transfer" from one kind of teaching to the other. In particular the aspects of quality control, cumulative improvement and staff development, can affect on-campus as well as off-campus teaching.

It is already happening in a half hidden way. Distance education materials are used by lecturers in traditional universities and colleges to prepare their own teaching. If I present the evidence for this in anecdotal form, it is because the matter is not, to my knowledge, documented. It is part of the *demimonde* of education. It is not illegal, it is not plagiarism, but nobody cares to document it.

The anecdote runs as follows. I have often been complimented on the quality of Deakin study guides. "I use them myself." a lecturer tells me. "They are so well structured." I explain that a lot of effort went into preparing them. They are not the work of an individual but the products of course teams. They have been subjected to peer criticism and an instructional designer has had a say before they go into print. "Do you give them to your students?" I ask. That idea has never occurred to the lecturer. "Oh no—I just use them in preparing my lectures." The lecturer is paid to give lectures. I can't blame anybody for operating according to the hallowed norms of the profession.

When the study guides are overtly used for on-campus teaching, there can be major cost advantages. The economies of scale can be increased by using the materials that are produced for off-campus students to teach on-campus and off-campus students as well. This is what Deakin University did, but the potential is much greater than was realized in that case, within the student body of one relatively small university (some 7,000 students).

A UTOPIAN FUTURE

I look forward to a culmination of the trends I have described in a frankly utopian vision of the future. In this idyllic state of affairs, all subject matter will be available in a choice of modes. Whatever students want to study they will be able to do it in a choice of modes—by campus-based lectures and tutorials or through printed study guides or by audio tapes or by interactive video and so on. Naturally they will also be able to combine these modes in any kind of mixture that they wish.

Thus the students will become empowered to a degree hitherto unimaginable. Education systems at present are characterized predominantly by producer sovereignty. In this utopian future that I imagine, the consumer will reign. It won't matter if students want to delay their education. Retention rates in secondary school might still be a social problem, but they will no longer be an education problem. Lifelong learning will be as feasible as it is possible to make it because people will be able to learn when, where and how they like.

When I initially advanced the case for parity of esteem for distance education, I argued that its inherent differences conferred on it a pattern of advantages different from those associated with campus-based education, and that sufficient educational value resulted that one could no longer hold to the old prejudice of distance education being second rate. However, as the boundaries between distance education and campus based education have become increasingly blurred, I have wondered "Is the parity argument being superceded?" (Jevons, 1987, p. 19). It has seemed to me, as I have described it here, that ". . .the two modes will become more like each other both in the methods they use and in the clientele they serve" (Jevons, 1987, p. 19). I viewed the open learning movement as evidence of the convergence of methods. I believe the clienteles the two modes serve will converge more so than has been the case to date as the artificial barriers that have been imposed continue to break down. In large part this will occur because of the pressures that exist in many countries for more educational demand than the educational systems of these nations can provide.

Although there are encouraging and substantial signs that convergence is occurring, it will take some while yet before convergence can truly be recognized as having occurred. However, it does seem clear that the further convergence proceeds, ". . .the more the question of parity becomes emptied of significance" (Jevons, 1987, p. 20).

REFERENCES

Anwyl, J., Powles, M. and Patrick, K. (1986). *Who uses external studies? Who should?* Report to the Standing Committee on External Studies, Commonwealth Tertiary Education Commission, Canberra.

Commonwealth Tertiary Education Commission (1988). *Review of Efficiency and effectiveness in higher education,* Australian Government Publishing Service, Canberra.

Foks, J. (1987). Towards open learning. In P. Smith and M. Kelly (Eds.), *Distance Education and the Mainstream.* Croom Helm, London.

Jevons, F. (1979). How different is the distance student? Paper presented to the Open University Conference on the Education of Adults at a Distance, Birmingham, 1979.

Jevons, F. (1982) How different is the distance student? In J.S. Daniel, M. A. Stroud and J. R. Thompson (Eds.), *Learning at a Distance;* Edmonton: Athabasca University/International Council for Correspondence Education.

Jevons, F. (1984) Distance education in mixed institutions: working towards parity. *Distance Education;* 5(1); 24–37.

Jevons, F. (1987) Distance education and campus-based education: parity of esteem. In P. Smith and M. Kelly (Eds.) *Distance Education and the Mainstream.* Croom Helm; New York.

Keegan, D. and Rumble, G. (1982). Distance teaching at university level. In G. Rumble and K. Harry (Eds.). *The Distance Teaching Universities.* London, Croom Helm.

Smith, P. (1987). Distance education and educational change. In P. Smith and M. Kelly (Eds.), *Distance Education and the Mainstream.* Croom Helm, London.

Woodley, A. and MacIntosh, N. (1980). *The door stood open: An evaluation of the Open University younger student pilot scheme,* Open University, Milton Keynes.